Energy and Industry

The Potential of Energy Development Projects for Canadian Industry in the Eighties

The Canadian Institute for Economic Policy has been established to engage in public discussion of fiscal, industrial and other related public policies designed to strengthen Canada in a rapidly changing international environment.

The Institute fulfills this mandate by sponsoring and undertaking studies pertaining to the economy of Canada and disseminating such studies. Its intention is to contribute in an innovative way to the development of public policy in Canada.

Other titles available in the Canadian Institute for Economic Policy Series are:

The Monetarist Counter-Revolution: A Critique of Canadian Monetary Policy 1975-1979
Arthur W. Donner and Douglas D. Peters

Canada's Crippled Dollar: An Analysis of International Trade and Our Troubled Balance of Payments
H. Lukin Robinson

Unemployment and Inflation: The Canadian Experience
Clarence L. Barber and John C. P. McCallum

How Ottawa Decides: Planning and Industrial Policy-Making 1968-1980
Richard D. French

Canadian Institute for Economic Policy
Suite 409 350 Sparks St., Ottawa K1R 7S8

Energy and Industry

The Potential of Energy Development Projects for Canadian Industry in the Eighties

Barry Beale

Canadian Institute for Economic Policy

The opinions expressed in this study are those of the author alone and are not intended to represent those of any organization with which he may be associated.

ISBN 0-88862-408-5 cloth
ISBN 0-88862-407-7 paper
6 5 4 3 2 1   80 81 82 83 84 85 86

Canadian Cataloguing in Publication Data
  Beale, Barry, 1949-
    Energy and industry

  (Industrial strategies series)

  ISBN 0-88862-407-7 pa.   ISBN 0-88862-408-5 bd.

1. Energy development - Canada. 2. Energy industries - Canada. 3. Energy policy - Canada. I. Canadian Institute for Economic Policy. II. Title. III. Series.

HD9502.C32B42   333.79′15′0971   C80-094834-3

Additional copies of this book
may be purchased from:

James Lorimer & Company, Publishers
Egerton Ryerson Memorial Building
35 Britain Street,
Toronto M5A 1R7, Ontario

Printed and bound in Canada

61,410

Contents

Tables and Charts

Foreword

The key words in the current energy policy debate are price, availability, self-sufficiency and so on. Industrial development is rarely mentioned.

However, the massive investment in energy development projected for the 1980s—anywhere from $200 to over $300 billion—provides major industrial opportunities for Canadian industry. Moreover, these opportunities are presenting themselves at a time when Canada is said to be "de-industrializing." Energy development gives us a chance to restructure our industrial base to meet the new challenges of international trade.

Barry Beale's assessment of the industrial opportunities related to proposed energy projects provides a much needed overview. The Institute is publishing this study to indicate to Canadians that, at a time when there is so much concern about our economic future, there are major opportunities to stimulate industrial development and economic growth. It is up to us to seize these opportunities. Others are waiting in the wings to do so. The policy directions outlined in this study should be actively discussed by our decision-makers.

This study is the first in the Institute's Industrial Strategy Series. Like all our commissioned studies, the views expressed here are those of the author and do not necessarily reflect those of the Institute.

R.D. Voyer
Executive Director
Canadian Institute for Economic Policy

Introduction

This study has a somewhat different approach from that usually taken when energy and industrial activity are under discussion. Rather than assessing the impact of ever-increasing energy prices on Canadian firms, this study is concerned with the role Canadian industry will play in the unparalleled development opportunities the energy sector offers over the next decade.

Investment in the energy sector over the next decade will be enormous: $210 billion is the figure suggested in this study; over $400 billion has been predicted by other observers. This represents an investment of three times as much in the next ten years as all energy investment over the past twenty. Problems of financing and staging these developments will be inevitable, but with the problems come immense benefits. The more salient of these include: providing Canadians with a more secure energy future; the associated spending in the construction, manufacturing and service-related sectors; and the opportunity to create thousands of new jobs. These benefits will be maximized if we ensure that the highest attainable proportion of energy-related, capital goods requirements are produced in Canada. This will have some beneficial results, in addition to those already mentioned:

- decreasing manufacturing trade and balance of payments deficits;
- facilitating regional economic development;
- stimulating Canadian innovation and export markets.

The maximization of Canadian participation in energy developments is a widely shared goal. What has been lacking, however, is an assessment of how well Canadian industry is in fact performing when matched against the requirements of the energy industry. Such an assessment is a primary objective of this study. From it, both the problems and opportunities come more clearly into focus.

Supplying equipment and services to the energy industry is no novel demand to Canadian industry. The Canadian experience in pipelining, electric utilities, and finding and developing oil and gas supplies has a long history in this country. The ability of Canadian industry to capture equipment orders and supply the associated services has incrementally improved over time. Those firms serving the utilities and the pipelines, in particular, have performed more than creditably in supplying equipment and machinery in response to diverse and exacting requirements.

There can be no complacency here, however. A new generation of energy projects is emerging that will require investment in energy sources novel to the Canadian experience. The oil sands, heavy oil upgrading, and offshore and frontier oil and gas exploration in hostile environments pose technological challenges, the solutions to which are only now being worked out. The next decade will see much emphasis being placed on new technologies, most of which will require highly sophisticated equipment, requirements that in many cases can only be satisfied by a few manufacturing firms in the world or by already established international competition. Maintaining a significant "Canadian content" for these new projects will require a concerted effort by both government and industry. One outcome may be a slow slide into increased foreign dependence for equipment; a more favourable development would see Canadians seizing the domestic opportunity, gaining experience and becoming global exporters of knowledge, technology and equipment.

A combination of both these new and rapidly expanding existing markets will challenge Canadian industry over the next decade. It will not occur in a vacuum. Not only must industry be willing to face the challenge, but governments must be willing to play a supportive role by encouraging entry into new fields and ensuring that the preconditions for Canadian involvement are present. The outcome will depend on the interplay between industry risk-taking and government provisions to mitigate that risk.

Proponents of anticipated energy projects have proclaimed their intention to accommodate the concern of government and Canadian industry that the preponderance of benefit from their investment remain in Canada. Somewhat less emphasis has been placed on how this will be accomplished and how far the effort will extend. These benefits must extend beyond equipment and labour requirements, to encompass the technology itself. The sheer diversity of the energy opportunities in this country could give Canada a distinct advantage in world trade. If the benefits from these opportunities are to be maximized, we must ensure the technologies used are indigenous.

The energy services industries are eager to become involved, but many are wary of the risk attached. For many, the investment in plant capacity, staffing requirements and changes to marketing approaches is large, relative to the uncertainty of the reward. Some must face parent companies located outside the country, who are often reluctant to allow their branch plants to evolve outside the traditional domestic markets. In addition, the specialized nature of many components often requires more outlets than a domestic market, even a protected domestic market, in order to achieve the requisite economies of scale.

One fact should be remembered. Energy developments are not unique to Canada but are global. Canadians must be well prepared to capitalize not only on our domestic opportunities, which are considerable, but also on opportunities to be found around the world.

Energy and Investment: Past and Future

1

Canada has entered the 1980s with a large degree of uncertainty about what our energy future will hold for the next decade and beyond. Compared to other countries we hold some significant natural resource advantages. While other countries are squeezed between a lack of domestic resources and an increasingly unstable foreign source of energy supply, the uncertainty in Canada stems from making decisions about which of our substantial domestic resources will be developed, to what degree, at what costs, and under whose control. Difficult questions to be sure, but they can, for the most part, be resolved within our borders.

A quick glance across the country shows energy opportunities of every type extending into virtually every region. In the North are the Foothills Yukon natural gas pipeline, the oil and gas discoveries in the Beaufort sea, the Mackenzie Valley and the High Arctic. In British Columbia future developments in coal, hydro and natural gas are planned. In Alberta new discoveries of conventional oil and gas, the tar sands, heavy oil, enhanced recovery and coal will ensure that province's prominent role in the Canadian energy future. In Saskatchewan there are heavy oil and uranium discoveries. Manitoba has massive hydro reserves. In Ontario there is uranium, the CANDU nuclear system and the opportunity of developing liquid fuels from the forest resource. In Quebec massive hydro potential is still being developed, and the main East/West natural gas pipeline is being extended at least as far as Quebec City. In Newfoundland preliminary engineering for the second phase of the Churchill Falls power project is underway and hopes are high that offshore oil from Hibernia will prove a reality. New Brunswick will commission a new nuclear station in 1981. Natural gas has been discovered off the coast of Nova Scotia, and Fundy tidal power may yet be developed. And, finally, Prince Edward Island is leading the country in defining a conserver ethic and in developing renewable sources of wind, solar and biomass energy.

And yet, the uncertainty persists—in part because of the sheer diversity of the opportunities and in part because as a nation we have not yet crystallized the determination to get on with the job. Getting on with the job will require well coordinated policies with clear long- and short-term signals to the energy industry and to the manufacturing and financial communities if the technical, financial and industrial resources of the country are to be mobilized to achieve these energy goals.

It is particularly difficult to accurately forecast energy developments in Canada over the next ten to twenty years. This is a very dynamic area at present, with considerable change and adjustment from month to month: every day a new project or scheme seems to appear or be dropped from contention. As will be seen later in this chapter, this difficulty is very pronounced among forecasts of energy investment over the next decade. To this diversity of existing estimates this study adds its own, based on projects for which there have been or are likely to be commitments for the 1980s.

Whatever the ultimate form the project lists take over the next decade, several things are clear:

- The amounts of capital required will be staggering, from a minimum of $200 billion to as high as $400 billion, depending on the estimate used.
- There will be significant opportunities for Canadian firms to supply the equipment, machinery and service needs for these projects.
- Equipment needs will be highly diverse and specialized.
- There are many steps necessary to maximize Canadian industry's opportunity to supply these specialized requirements.

Capital-spending estimates are discussed in more detail in the following pages, while the other considerations will form the basis of the remaining chapters. Before a discussion of future project and expenditure lists, however, it will be useful to set the stage by highlighting several observations on past domestic consumption of the primary energy sources and identifying what energy sources are likely to be of most interest over the next decade.

Demand/Supply Overview

Over the past thirty years, consumption has increased at an average of 4.5 per cent per year, with petroleum and natural gas dominating.

Consumption of primary energy sources in Canada has increased steadily from 2.5 Quads (1 Quad = 1,000 trillion Btu) in 1950 to over 8.5 Quads in 1978, roughly a quarter of this growth occurring in the 1970s.[1] As shown graphically in Chart 1-1, petroleum and natural gas

TABLE 1-1
PROPORTION OF PRIMARY ENERGY CONSUMPTION
IN CANADA, 1950 – 78*

Year	Total Demand (Quads)	Coal and Coke (%)	Hydroelectric Power (%)	Nuclear Power (%)	Natural Gas (%)	Petroleum (%)
1950	2.49	47.6	20.1	—	2.5	29.8
1955	3.19	22.7	22.7	—	3.9	45.7
1960	3.17	14.7	27.1	—	9.0	48.6
1965	4.81	13.0	24.5	—	13.1	49.4
1970	6.33	10.7	24.6	0.1	16.5	48.1
1975	7.83	8.0	24.9	1.5	18.8	46.8
1978	8.52	8.8	25.2	3.5	18.5	44.0
Annual growth in actual consumption (Quads) (1950-1978)	4.5 %	(1.6%)	5.4%	—	12.4%	6.0%

*Adapted from *Energy Future for Canadians*, Department of Energy, Mines and Resources, Report EP 78-1, 1978.

3

CHART 1-1
RELATIVE IMPORTANCE
OF ENERGY SOURCES

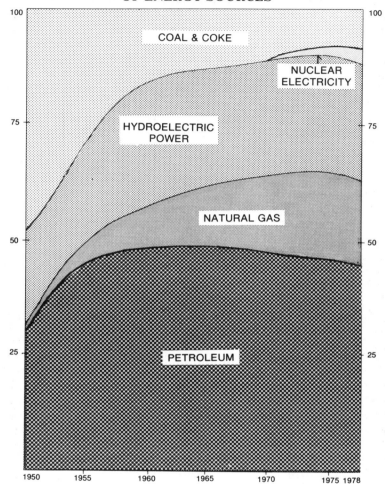

Source: Department of Energy, Mines and Resources, *Energy Future for Canadians*, Report EP 78-1, 1978.

have played an increasing role as primary energy sources, accounting for over 60 per cent of total primary energy demand over the past decade.

Coal and coke, although once major sources of energy, have

dropped to under 9 per cent of total primary energy demands, increasingly being substituted by oil and gas. Owing to the long distances between the principal producers (in the West) and the principal consumers (in the East), much of the coal has in fact been imported from sources in the United States. Although coal imports for 1978 were thirteen million tonnes, imports and exports have recently balanced, leaving Canada a small net exporter. Coal as a proportion of total consumption should increase as utilities and several industries switch to thermal coals, although the timing of these transitions is uncertain.

Hydroelectric power has increased its share of primary energy production to slightly over 25 per cent of the total. Many of our major watercourses have been developed, but there is still good potential in the lower James Bay, lower Churchill Falls and several sites in B.C. The Northwest Territories still has considerable untapped resources. Many smaller streams in Canada could add incrementally to existing hydro facilities.

Petroleum and natural gas have grown strongly and are 44 per cent and 18.5 per cent respectively of our total primary consumption (although petroleum has dropped from the high of 50 per cent in 1965). From 1947 Canada underwent a transition from a country importing 90 per cent of its petroleum to one of near self-reliance in 1968 when imports and exports were balanced. During the 1970s, however, Canada again became a net importer. Although in 1978 Canada in fact imported roughly 18 per cent less than in 1972, due to rising international prices we paid 410 per cent more for this oil. More domestic production is used now in domestic markets. Our exports of petroleum fell from 54.2 million m³ in 1972 to 15.6 million m³ in 1978.

The level of domestic consumption has been maintained at the expense of established reserves, however. In the period between 1951 and 1969, established reserves grew at an average annual rate of 12 per cent; annual additions consistently outpaced production. Between 1969 and 1978, however, total additions to proved reserves totalled 225 million m³, yet production totalled 774 million m³; the difference has come from reserves. In effect, Canada has consumed (without replacing), 35 per cent of peak 1969 reserves. At current production rates, between ten to eleven years of established conventional oil reserves remain.

Contrasted to this bleak picture for oil, natural gas shows exactly the opposite outlook. Except for a brief period during the 1960s, Canada has been a *net* exporter of substantial volumes of natural gas. In 1978 exports of 25 million m³ of gas worth $2.1 billion were recorded against a negligible amount of imports. Reserves of marketable gas increased

5

steadily up to the early Seventies and moderately thereafter. Between 1969 and 1978 total additions to marketable reserves were 0.9 trillion m³ while production totalled 0.6 trillion m³ and reserves grew by 10 per cent.[2]

The next ten years should see lower overall growth in demand, a shift in the primary energy mix and a few new sources. The most recent estimates by the National Energy Board (NEB) indicate a rate of growth in primary energy consumption of 3.4 per cent over the next decade, or roughly 25 per cent lower than the average for the previous thirty years. As shown in Table 1-2, an expanded role for gas, coal and primary electricity is anticipated.

TABLE 1-2
NATIONAL ENERGY BOARD ENERGY BALANCES IN 1990

	EMR *1978* *(actual %)*	*NEB* *1990* *(forecast %)*	*NEB* *1990* *(forecast-Quads)*
Oil	44.0	34.8	4.45
Gas and propane	18.5	20.7	2.65
Coal	8.8	9.8	1.25
Primary electricity	28.7	33.9	4.34
Other (from renew- able resources)	—	0.8	0.10
Total	100.0	100.0	12.79

Source: National Energy Board, *Canadian Oil and Gas Supply/Demand Overview*, November 1979.

A dramatic reduction occurs in the role of oil. Since there has been no major proven oil discovery since the mid-1960s, established reserves can be expected to continue falling. Based on existing information, the NEB estimate is that by 1990 Canada could face a domestic shortfall of 709,000 barrels/day or somewhat more than twice current imports. This is speculative, of course, and the current possibilities of significant oil finds in the Beaufort sea, High Arctic or the East Coast offshore may substantially alter these import requirements. Aside from the possibility of new discoveries, several new technologies and extraction systems will contribute to stretching out our oil resources:

- Oil sands deposits are very promising in terms of supply potential. In fact, the NEB estimates these sources will supply at least as much, if not more, oil than established conventional reserves of light crude by 1990.

- Heavy oil deposits, as the name suggests, contain thick oil that flows very poorly, although somewhat better than the tar sands. Through various extraction techniques this oil is encouraged to move more freely. Improvements in production technologies may allow in the order of 15 per cent of the total oil production in 1990 from these deposits.
- Enhanced oil recovery (EOR) techniques are constantly improving the total yield of existing reservoirs. Oil reservoirs are volumes of porous rock holding water, oil and gas under pressure. Primary production is accomplished by displacing oil toward the surface by natural pressure differences in the reservoir. Eventually, pressure declines occur and secondary recovery is implemented. These techniques generally involve fluid injection that increases pressure and drives more oil to the producing well. Economic limits of the technology, however, leave roughly *two-thirds* of the original oil in place, even after secondary treatment. Expensive tertiary recovery techniques are being developed that may extend reservoir producibility from a minimum of 8 per cent to a maximum of 48 per cent of established conventional oil reserves.[3] As oil prices at the well head rise, the economics of these enhanced recovery techniques become much more promising, subject, of course, to the royalty and tax regimes imposed on the industry.

Whether new oil is found or reservoir life extended, the effect will be to offset imported oil requirements. However, oil in 1990 will play a less significant role in our national energy balance than it has over the past twenty years.

Natural gas will play a much more prominent role over the next decade, given the surpluses currently available. Considerable effort is underway to encourage fuel switching, away from oil to gas for stationary energy uses, to increase domestic demand.

An expanded role for primary electricity can also be anticipated as a strategy for limiting oil consumption. Estimates by the Department of Energy, Mines and Resources suggest an increase in the order of 46 per cent in installed generating capacity by 1987, with the following breakdown of increases: hydro—15,565 megawatts; nuclear—10,820 megawatts; conventional thermal—6,096 megawatts; for total additions to capacity of 32,461 megawatts.[4] Hydro additions will include new capacity at James Bay, the lower Churchill Falls, at Gull Island and committed programs within British Columbia.

Nuclear plans, although somewhat unclear, will show some activity with the completion of projects already committed. The above estimate includes nuclear stations at Point LePreau in New Brunswick, Darlington and Bruce 2 in Ontario, and Gentilly 2 in Quebec. The post-Darlington order books are empty, however, and the future of nuclear energy in the late Eighties and Nineties is very uncertain.

Non-nuclear thermal generating plants will increasingly use coal, the greatest expansion occurring in Alberta, Saskatchewan and the Maritimes.

TABLE 1-3
POTENTIAL CONTRIBUTIONS OF INDIVIDUAL
TECHNOLOGIES IN FUTURE PRIMARY ENERGY SUPPLY

	1975	1985	2000
		(Quads)	
Non-renewable Technologies			
Oil and gas—exploration	0	—	5.2
Crude oil—production	3.5	2.4	1.3
Natural gas—production	2.25	2.8	2.4
Crude oil—enhanced recovery	—	.08	.4
Natural gas—enhanced recovery and expansion	—	.05	.15
Heavy oils—production and enhanced recovery	—	.1	.2
Oil sands—mining	.1	.85	2
Oil sands—in situ	.01	.2	1
Coal—direct utilization	.1	.4	1.4
Coal—conversion to liquid or gaseous fuels	—	—	.01
Nuclear Energy Technologies			
Nuclear—fission	.06	.4	2.1
"Renewable" Energy Technologies			
Hydroelectricity	.7	1.1	1.5
Energy from biomass and solid wastes	.12	.42	.98
Solar space and water heating	—	.1	.4
Solar electric power	0	0	—
Geothermal energy	(.0006)	.002	.05
Wind energy	—	.004	.016
Tidal power	0	—	.02
Total	6.85	8.91	19.13

Source: Science Council of Canada, *Roads to Energy Self-Reliance*, Report 30, June 1979.

Renewable energy technologies, other than hydro, will receive increasing attention over the next decade. Even according to the most optimistic projections, however, they will account for not much more than 8 per cent of primary energy demand by the year 2000. Estimates by the Science Council indicate that the greatest energy opportunities are in biomass and solid waste, which by 2000 could possibly account for 0.98 Quads out of a total demand for 19.13 Quads.

Energy Investment Trends

Capital investment by the energy sector, as a proportion of total Canadian investment, has increased substantially over the past twenty years, but the investment mix has remained relatively uniform.

The significance of the perceived energy opportunity in Canada is best illustrated by the fact that over 20 per cent of all domestic capital investment is currently spent by the energy sector. In contrast, in the period 1961 – 65, energy sector investment was an average 13 per cent of total capital investment. As shown in Chart 1-2, the Seventies saw a dramatic increase in the absolute dollar volume of investment: in fact, the energy sector invested more money (in current dollars) in 1977 and 1978 alone than was invested in the entire decade of the Sixties. Further, as reflected in Chart 1-2, the oil and gas industry and the utilities accounted for 87 per cent of all investment in 1978, up from 76 per cent in the five-year period from 1961 to 1965.

Expenditures by the electric utilities have historically been greater by far than any other sector, representing, on average, 55 per cent of energy sector investment over the past twenty years. Expenditures have increased in the order of 14 per cent per year, from $691 million a year in the 1961 – 65 period to $6.1 billion in 1978, with some variation in annual growth rates, depending on the timing of expenditures for large hydro or nuclear facilities.

The crude petroleum and natural gas sector has been the second largest energy investor, representing 25 per cent of capital expenditures on energy over the past twenty years. Although sporadic, the sector has averaged a 13 per cent annual growth rate from an annual average of $335 million invested in the 1961 – 65 period to over $2.7 billion in 1978. The figures noted are for capital expenditures on drilling, equipment and construction of natural gas plants, which in 1978 represented only 30 per cent of total *cash* expenditures by the industry. If royalties, operating expenses and land acquisition are included, the total cash outlay for 1978 was $8.7 billion, compared to $710 million in 1961. The rate of growth for oil and gas investments has been particularly rapid in the latter part of the Seventies, averaging between 28 to 30 per cent per year.

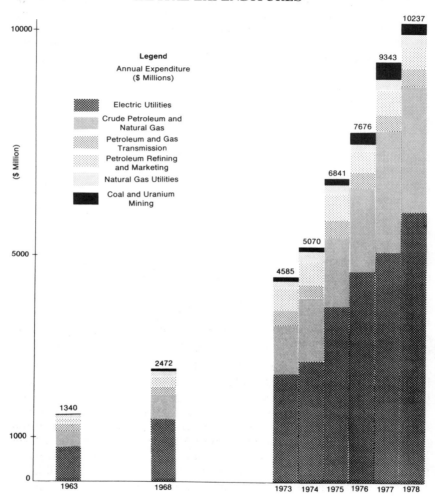

CHART 1-2
PATTERN OF CANADIAN ENERGY SECTOR
CAPITAL EXPENDITURES

Legend

Annual Expenditure
($ Millions)

Electric Utilities

Crude Petroleum and
Natural Gas

Petroleum and Gas
Transmission

Petroleum Refining
and Marketing

Natural Gas Utilities

Coal and Uranium
Mining

Source: Statistics Canada, *Private and Public Investment in Canada*, Catalogue 61-205.

Pipeline investment, although growing at an average annual rate of 6.7 per cent since the early Sixties, has declined as a proportion of investment from 9.2 per cent in 1961 to under 4 per cent in 1978. The Sixties and early Seventies were periods of high construction activity

10

as the major oil and gas trunk lines were put in place across the country. Activity through the latter part of the Seventies has been geared mainly to the construction of feeder lines and the looping of the main line with a few large single projects. Several proposals are being considered, which, if successful, will boost the significance of the pipeline industry: including the Foothills Yukon natural gas pipeline, the Polar Gas Pipeline and the recently approved Montreal to Quebec City gas link.

The remaining investment in the energy sector has historically constituted less than 10 per cent of the total:

- Petroleum refining and marketing represented 4.5 per cent in 1978, down from an 11 per cent high in 1974. Of the thirty-eight refineries across the country, only five were commissioned in the Seventies and only one since 1975. Most expenditures for refineries in the past decade have involved the upgrading or expansion of facilities.

- Coal and uranium mining, although still small (3 per cent of the total investment in 1978), has shown explosive growth since the early Sixties: over 25 per cent per year on average, from $6 million invested per year from 1961 to 1965 to $331 million in 1978. Most of this growth has occurred in uranium mining, primarily for export markets and secondly to satisfy domestic demands for the CANDU nuclear system.

- Investment in renewable energy sources other than hydro has been negligible, although biomass, in the form of mill waste, is becoming an increasingly important source of energy within the forestry industry.

Energy Investment Forecasts

Over the past few years, energy investment forecasts have been developed by governments, oil companies, associations and financial institutions, as well as other groups. Most of these forecasts have been modelled from the top down: the future investment profile has been estimated based upon a series of macro-assumptions with some structural relationships built into the model. While many are sophisticated attempts with hundreds of intricate relationships, the variation in possible assumptions, the range of methodologies employed and the different degrees of comprehensiveness make these forecasts incommensurable with each other. Some examples: total energy investment forecasts for 1980 – 90 (in constant 1980 dollars) have been made by Energy, Mines and Resources ($216 – 221 billion);[5] investment analyst A.E. Ames ($320 – 412 billion);[6] and the Canadian Petroleum Association ($218.5 – 242.8 billion).[7]

These forecasts are useful in their own context, but their major limitation is failure to specify (or sometimes even to consider) actual projects and their timing.

Another approach to forecasting is to work from the bottom up, building totals based on committed or likely projects. Since very few attempts to relate total capital expenditures to actual projects have been made in the past, this is the approach that has been adopted for the purposes of this study. While it appears to be conservative, most major projects to be undertaken during the 1980s should already be at least in the conceptual stage, given the long lead times necessitated by regulatory, financing and construction requirements. The approach of filling in the base of the information pyramid and working upward should at least yield a minimum level of investment by 1990. The result is an anticipated investment of $210 billion between 1980 and 1990, as broken down in Table 1-4. Data on committed and proposed projects were collected from a wide variety of trade journals, government documents and corporate statements. Lists were developed, and during the course of interviews with knowledgeable observers of and participants in the energy industry, subjective estimates and comments were incorporated. As an estimate, however, Table 1-4 should be viewed with some caution. Some significant limitations include the following:

- The effect of energy pricing has not been specifically addressed nor has the central policy issue of whether Canada should be self-reliant (balanced oil and gas imports and exports) or self-sufficient (no oil imports). The scope of this report has not allowed discussion of optimum strategies to attain either of these two objectives. Should a national energy development strategy be adopted over the next few years, the investment profile could be markedly different from that indicated in this study. Some observers, for example, advocate a much expanded role for tar sands development and a diminished role for offshore and frontier exploration programs, based on the apparent poor contribution of these latter regions in increasing supplies over the past decade.[8]

- Cost of financing has not always been included (depending on the source) but the ability to finance has been assumed. Most industry observers suggest financing should be available.

- Pipeline expenditures do not include the Polar Gas project, which if approved is assumed to occur after 1990.

- Oil and gas exploration and production are not project related and must be estimated. Estimates for producing regions are conservatively assumed at a 5 per cent real growth rate in capital expenditures for drilling and equipment, based on 1979 estimates. Cash

12

TABLE 1-4
FORECAST CAPITAL EXPENDITURES IN THE ENERGY
SECTOR, 1980 – 90

	Cumulative Expenditure by 1990 (million 1980 $'s)		Proportion* of Total (%)
Utilities	63,300		30
Thermal generation		8,400	4
Hydroelectric		34,000	16
Nuclear & heavy water		11,900	6
Transmission		9,000	4
Oil and Gas Related	135,000		64
Exploration & development			
Producing regions		42,000	20
Enhanced recovery		700	**
Frontiers		48,000	23
Tar sands/Heavy oil		21,900	10
Refineries and gas plants		5,000	2
Pipelines		17,400	8
Uranium Mining/Processing	1,200		**
Coal Mining	5,000		2
Alternative Energy	5,000		2
Total	209,500		

* May not equal 100 due to rounding.
** Less than 1%.

expenditures including royalties, land acquisition and operating expenses would be much higher. Investment in frontier areas has assumed a substantial increase in annual investment for exploration and uses North Sea exploration development ratios. Industry observers suggest that $48 billion is an acceptable figure. Depending on the selling price of oil and the volume of oil discovered, investment could be either much less or much more.

- Electric utilities expenditures may be understated since no explicit allowance for rapid growth in electrical consumption, either in an effort to displace heating oil or through policies to export electricity to the United States, has been assumed. If either of these

13

conditions prevail and if a commitment to nuclear power is made, the forecast $63 billion could be much higher.

Based on these forecasts, the mix of investment will be somewhat different from that of the past decade. In relation to the total, the oil and gas industry and electric utilities will still dominate with 80 per cent of total investment. Their roles will be reversed, however, with proportionately more money invested by the petroleum exploration and development programs than by the utilities for new plants.

Electric utilities could in fact represent only 30 per cent of total investment between 1980 and 1990 compared to 55 per cent in 1978. Uncertainties about the rate of demand increase for this period are creating conservative investment attitudes on future projects in many utilities. In addition, the nuclear industry component of the forecast assumes no new orders, only the clearing of existing commitments. Towards the end of the decade there may in fact be no nuclear investment activity at all if new orders are not forthcoming. Included within the nuclear forecast are: the completion of Gentilly 2 in Quebec, Pickering B, Bruce B and Darlington in Ontario, for a total addition to capacity of 9,600 megawatts. Two others are in limbo and not included: the second phase of Point LePreau in New Brunswick and Gentilly 3 in Quebec.

Hydroelectric expansion is dominated by twenty identified projects in Quebec and twelve in British Columbia, out of a total of forty-two projects. Assuming no delays, addition to capacity is in the order of 55,000 megawatts. Of this total, 15 – 20,000 megawatts may not be completed before 1990.

Investment in thermal generating stations is almost exclusively based on coal and concentrated in Nova Scotia, Alberta, Saskatchewan and Ontario. A total of nineteen projects have been identified with additions to capacity of 13,200 megawatts. Four small diesel, gas turbine and peat-fired projects were also identified but represent only an additional 400 megawatts.

Oil- and gas-related investment will become much more prominent in the 1980s as production programs in the frontiers and along the East Coast are accelerated. Costs of these programs will be well above traditional levels as challenges posed by harsh environments, remote locations and new technologies are met and overcome. *In situ* recovery and mining of oil sands will receive increasing attention. Optimistically (given uncertainties on oil-pricing agreements which affect these projects), four projects (Alsands, Cold Lake and two others) could be possible by the end of the decade, plus the anticipated expansions at Syncrude and the Great Canadian Oil Sands projects.

14

As the transportation and distribution of oil and gas from northern locations gain more credibility in the 1980s, investment in pipeline transmission systems will be heavier than over the past decade, representing roughly 8 per cent of total investment compared to under 1 per cent in 1978. The major expenditure will be for the Foothills Yukon natural gas pipeline (at $12 – 14 billion). Also included are the expansion of main lines to the Maritimes, the Foothills Dempster lateral, and the Arctic Pilot project that proposes to bring liquified natural gas (LNG) from the Arctic islands. Several other more modest oil and gas extensions and replacements have also been included. Not included are the Polar Gas project (assumed to be post-1990) and investment in distribution systems.

Uranium and coal mining, refineries and alternative energy investments make up the balance, accounting for 7 per cent of forecast expenditures. Uranium and coal mining represent a modest gain as a proportion of investment, from 3 per cent in 1978 to 4 per cent by 1990. New uranium refineries in Ontario and Saskatchewan, the development of new deposits and the expansion of existing operations in Saskatchewan, Ontario and Newfoundland are anticipated. The full extent of coal mining is uncertain but promising, given expanded export opportunities and the increasing use of coal in the utilities expansion programs. Investment is confined to B.C., Alberta and Nova Scotia.

Refining expenditures will continue to decline in importance over the study period. Only one major new refinery, processing synthetic crude from the tar sands, has been proposed to date. Many much smaller additions to capacity can be expected across the country, and half-a-dozen major upgrading projects are likely, as various refineries extend refining capacity to the heavy and residual oils currently exported to U.S. markets.

Renewable energy sources, other than hydro, will receive increasing attention primarily in Ontario, Quebec and Prince Edward Island. Energy production systems from solid waste, peat and the forest are particularly promising. Co-generation and district heating projects are proposed in Ontario, and both Quebec and Ontario show strong interest in the gasification of wood to produce methanol to eventually replace gasoline. Ontario has suggested $16 billion as the investment required in renewables (solar and biomass) to contribute to 35 per cent energy self-sufficiency by 1995, an overly optimistic but indicative assessment of the role of renewables after 1990. Over the study period, however, investment in alternative energy sources will continue to be overwhelmed by more conventional energy investment programs.

Past and Future Manufacturing Performance

2

A minimum program of $210 billion over the next decade to develop Canadian energy supplies is a prospect staggering in its scope. This represents a 300 per cent increase in investment in ten years compared to the total for the past twenty. Equally staggering are the manpower, equipment and servicing requirements implied by such a program.

This chapter provides an overview of the ability of domestic industry to fulfill these requirements, highlighting equipment manufacture, but also commenting on service and engineering performance:

- First, industry's past performance in the major energy sectors is analysed by assessing the magnitude of equipment cost in relation to total project expenditures and estimating the level of Canadian content achieved.

- Second, the contribution Canadian firms may make is assessed for those project types (and their requirements) that are only just emerging as major energy sources and for which little or no practical experience is available.

- Finally, there is an overall assessment of the opportunity for Canadian firms to supply the requirements of the energy sector in the Eighties, with commentary on the problems to be overcome.

The development in each industry segment of the energy sector exhibits varying degrees of benefit to domestic industry, depending on the availability of technical and equipment requirements in Canada. Each raises issues peculiar to that segment.

Canadian Content

Throughout this study, reference will be made to the various energy segments achieving a specified level of Canadian content in procurement programs and in associated services such as engineering and

16

design. What in fact "Canadian content" means is subject to wide divergence of opinion. There are three alternative definitions, either used in practice or discussed in theory at the moment.

The first refers to a product or component as Canadian whenever the source of supply is located in Canada. This is the operating definition of most industries in Canada and is generally applied by energy sector proponents in descriptions of procurement programs for past projects. It is a highly misleading definition, however, since any product purchased through a Canadian supplier would qualify, even if the product was in fact manufactured in another country—in which case the only thing Canadian is the mark-up the distributor takes.

The second definition refers to a product as Canadian whenever the last point of manufacture is a domestic operation. Implied in the definition is the requirement that the last point be *substantial* in nature, although defining "substantial" can be as much a problem as defining "Canadian." As a definition, though, it is clearly preferable to the first, and it is the operating definition used within the European Economic Community. From all appearances, it is the definition most favoured in Alberta at the moment.

The third alternative is to make a more sophisticated attempt to identify and deduct the cost of imported components from the total manufactured cost of goods produced in Canada. Before a product could be stamped "Made in Canada" or "Product of Canada," a minimum level of Canadian content would have to be established. Setting this minimum poses several conceptual problems. If, for example, a level is set at 70 per cent and a product has only 60 per cent defined Canadian content, what is the status of the product? It cannot be called Canadian but at the same time it is clearly not a foreign product. A second problem area arises for those products having a high foreign content of raw materials not available in Canada, such as gold and diamonds for jewelry or imported cloth for textiles, for example. In this case the raw materials are transformed in a substantial way, yet the final product will exhibit low domestic content.[1] However these issues are resolved, this last definition would unquestionably be ideal for this study as it would allow not only purchases of 100 per cent foreign content to be isolated but also the level of foreign components in Canadian products. Research could then be conducted to identify clusters of imports and to focus recommendations on import substitution programs to be developed. The energy sector, however, does not generally collect information on procurement practices in this way, although there are some exceptions. Ontario Hydro, for example, in its "Buy Canadian" policy will typically investigate Canadian content to a depth of one supplier. The pipeline industry is another example. It performs its analysis in even greater depth—often as far as calculating the Canadian content of the coal used for the steel that in turn is used for the pipe! These are exceptions, however; the rule is to document only the source of manufacture. By necessity this is the definition generally used in this study. Any variation will be noted with explanatory comments. Each Canadian manufacturer will exhibit a somewhat different result for "value-added," based on the availability of Canadian components and corporate procurement policies. This topic will again be discussed in Chapter 3 in the context of its importance in defining procurement policies which maximize Canadian content.

Two Classes of Industrial Opportunities

To simplify the discussion of the industrial requirements for energy developments in the 1980s, two quite distinct categories of activity will be evident through the next decade and beyond. Opportunities will be geared towards:

- continuing to supply those energy sectors that have had a long and ongoing history of domestic development; or
- developing markets in those sectors that are only recent arrivals to the Canadian energy scene.

The previous chapter has identified over $75 billion which will be invested in projects that are new to Canadian and global experience: these will include oil sands and heavy oil where Canada is already a world leader; frontier and offshore field development; and the more promising of the renewable energy technologies. These sectors provide opportunities to develop an indigenous technology base with export potential. Maximizing Canadian participation *from the start* in these new markets will be vastly preferable to letting these opportunities slip into other hands.

Over the next decade, in the order of 63 per cent of energy investment will be in energy areas for which Canadian industry has evolved a degree of expertise in supplying: principally, the utilities; and the conventional oil and gas industry, including land-based field exploration, development, refining and pipeline construction. With over $81 billion invested in these areas over the past two decades, one would expect that Canadian firms would be more than capable in supplying their equipment and service requirements. Future manufacturing opportunities will consist in expanding production capacity to meet rapidly expanding equipment requirements, and in isolating those currently imported that could be manufactured in Canada.

Domestic Supplies for Oil/Gas Development

Excluding, for the moment, offshore exploratory and development programs and the oil sands projects, there are three areas in the conventional oil and gas industry where a significant amount of machinery, equipment and services are required: land-based drilling, and production; refining and processing; and pipeline construction. Requirements for each are quite different and the opportunities for domestic firms to supply their needs have evolved along very dissimilar paths.

Land-based drilling for oil and gas in Canada has a history stretching back to 1857 to the first successful oil strike at Oil Springs, Ontario. The following ninety years saw further activity, although limited production, in Ontario, Alberta and the Northwest Territories. The great turning point in Canadian crude oil production came with the major Alberta discoveries at the Leduc field in 1947 and at Redwater the following year. These finds set the stage for hundreds of other discoveries over the next thirty years. Since 1947 in the order of 100,000 exploratory wells have been drilled and total industry cash expenditures for all aspects of field development are estimated at $49 billion.[2] Given the long history and the high level of oil and gas exploration and development, one could expect that if there were a truly Canadian industry, drilling for oil and gas would be it.

Not all of the past and future expenditures of the industry represent opportunities for manufacturing. In fact, for every dollar spent in the full annual exploration, development and production programs of the industry, only twenty-six cents actually relate to drilling and equipment expenditures. The balance is spent on royalties, land and miscellaneous exploration, and operating categories. A representative breakdown of the petroleum industry's cash expenditures would approximate the following: royalties—39 per cent; drilling and field equipment—26 per cent; land acquisition—12 per cent; and others (including operating)—23 per cent.

Drilling for oil and gas requires some differentiation between the responsibilities of the oil company, which pays for drilling, and the contractor, who actually drills the well. For the most part, the activities of the oil companies are characterized by the high degree to which contractors are used to perform the pre-production functions of development. In this case, the oil company acquires the right to explore for oil and gas under a particular piece of land, selects locations, determines the depth to be drilled, selects and pays the contractor and decides to abandon or complete wells for production. The contractor is responsible for setting up by the "spud" date and drilling until the well is successful or abandoned. Other subcontracted companies, such

19

as those supplying mud, casings, cement and testing services, are employed directly by the operator.

Although each subcontractor has particular equipment requirements, the drilling rigs used by the drilling contractor make up the bulk of the capital expenditure on equipment. These rigs are a complex combination of specialized parts and machinery, using thousands of parts

TABLE 2-1
PRINCIPAL EQUIPMENT REQUIREMENTS
FOR DRILLING RIGS

Mast or Derrick:	Provides a rigid framework for raising and lowering drill pipe and casing.
Crown and Travelling Blocks:	Form a system of pulleys to raise and lower the weight of the drill pipe.
Draw-works:	Act as the transmission for the rig, reeling in or feeding off cable when raising and lowering the pipe. The draw-works are the heart of the rig and generally the largest and most expensive component. Its lifting capacity usually determines the depth rating of the rig.
Engines:	Generally diesel or diesel/electric to power the draw-works and auxiliary equipment.
Blowout Preventors:	Installed over the well head to seal the top of the well to prevent uncontrolled flow of gas, oil or drilling fluid.
Mud Pumps:	Used to pump a drilling fluid down the drill stem to the bit and return the fluid and rock cuttings to the surface.
Substructure:	The base for the derrick, draw-works and machinery.
Auxiliary:	Numbering in the hundreds, including a small generating plant, boilers, instrumentation and holding tanks for fluids.

from various suppliers. Seven classes of rigs, rated by a range of depth requirements, are necessary for land drilling, with manufacturing and fabrication costs ranging from $850,000 for rigs designed for shallow drilling up to 950 metres to over $5 million for rigs drilling to depths of over 4,600 metres. Each size of rig is generally identical in terms of equipment required, although in most cases the components are not interchangeable between the depth categories. Basic equipment for the rig is described in Table 2-1.

Drilling rigs are highly mobile pieces of equipment and are attracted to where the most favourable activity is occurring. Partly because of government incentives for oil and gas exploration over the past several years, Canada—Alberta in particular—has witnessed a very high level of drilling activity, with the contract drilling industry reaching new records every year since 1975. The result has been a steadily increasing supply of drilling rigs and an annual drilling capacity that has more than doubled in the last five years. (See Table 2-2.)

TABLE 2-2
ANNUAL DRILLING CAPACITY, CANADA

	1975	1979	1980 (estimate)	1981 (estimate)
Number of rigs	274	429	540	600
Number of wells drilled	4,200	7,800	9,900 (capacity)	10,900 (capacity)

Sources: Personal communication, Stanley Jones, Executive Director, Canadian Association of Oil Well Drilling Contractors, March 1980; also Department of Energy, Mines and Resources, *Oil and Natural Gas Industries in Canada*, Report ER 78-2, 1978.

So long as incentives are offered to the industry, this rate of growth is likely to continue. An example of the trans-national mobility of rigs was demonstrated between 1973 and 1975 when contractors were concerned with lack of federal support to their industry. During this time period over eighty rigs were reported as permanently removed to the larger and (at the time) more lucrative market in the United States. This diversion represented over one-quarter of the total stock of rigs as of that date.

Nonetheless, the record growth of the industry has led to a significant increase in the Canadian ability to supply components for the drilling rigs and production equipment. Estimates indicate that between 70 and 80 per cent of the equipment costs for these rigs are now sourced in Canada. This has not always been the case. According to officials of the Canadian Association of Oil Well Drilling Contractors, as recently as five years ago Canadian content was effectively zero, with rigs generally imported from the United States.

With demand for rigs expanding rapidly and no end in sight, there has been a recently exploited opportunity to engage in rig fabrication in Edmonton. Manufacturing rigs is no more complicated than knowing how to put the pieces together, and many of the pieces have always been available in Canada. With fabrication now taking place in Alberta, Canadian suppliers, particularly in that province, are much more likely to compete successfully against often much larger American firms. Proximity to the source of fabrication provides a natural competitive advantage, resulting in several components now being supplied by Canadians. A partial list of these includes:

- all structural steel requirements;
- derricks;
- substructure;
- wire rope;
- tanks.

Knowledgeable observers suggest that the current level of 80 per cent Canadian content represents a penetration that is unlikely to be exceeded in the near future. Several of the important equipment requirements are currently uneconomical to produce in Canada. It would appear that there is simply not enough demand, even now, in the Canadian market. The largest single market for land rigs is the United States with 2,500; Canada represents the next largest with just over 500; and there are perhaps only an additional 2,000 in the rest of the world. In any given year the total global requirements may be only 300 rigs, and this is split among seven different sizes of rigs. For Canadian requirements, even at the height of current activity, there may be no more than 12 to 15 rigs required for each size. Under these circumstances the larger more specialized equipment will continue to be imported unless Canadian manufacturers are willing to enter international markets often serviced by only a handful of firms. The most significant of current import requirements include the following:

- Draw-works, which are not interchangeable between rig sizes. Each size requires a production run much larger than Canadian requirements. Two or three large manufacturers in the United States are firmly established in the global market.
- Mud pumps which operate at 4,000—5,000 pounds pressure. They are not manufactured in Canada. Machinery cylinders for these pumps involve high technology and substantial investment. The market is very limited.

- Diesel engines. These are unavailable in Canada and will continue to be imported.

Peripheral equipment is supplied to the drilling industry by Canadian manufacturers. There are, for example, an estimated three thousand specialized tractor and trailer units to move drilling rigs between locations and as many again to haul mud, pipe and cement to the rigs, in addition to an uncounted number of pickup trucks.

Finally, the drilling process itself requires substantial amounts of materials that are consumed as drilling proceeds. Most of these "consumables" such as water, mud and cement are contracted by local suppliers. Other more sophisticated requirements are for seamless casing (2,100 metres for an average exploratory well and as much again for a producing well) and the heavy drill pipe itself. For the former, Canadian steel manufacturers in Eastern mills are capable of supplying all requirements. With 7,800 wells drilled in 1979, thousands of kilometres of casing material were required. Drill pipe, however, is not being manufactured in Canada. The pipe itself may be easily produced, but a world flash welding patent on the tool joint precludes the use of Canadian pipe. To date no manufacturer has applied to the holder of the U.S. patent to operate the process under license.

Refining and Processing Opportunities
Refining crude petroleum and processing raw natural gas for final markets have to keep pace with market demands throughout the country. Activity over the next decade will be geared to incremental additions in capacity as new discoveries are located and as the pattern of demand in the Eighties evolves.

There is currently oil-refining capacity in every province except Prince Edward Island, and as of 1978, thirty-eight refineries had a total installed capacity of over 364,000 m³/day of crude oil. As shown in Table 2-3, 75 per cent of this capacity has been in place since before 1970. Not surprisingly, the greatest growth in capacity occurred in the oil boom years between 1947 and 1960 when capacity expanded at a rate of 10.5 per cent annually; since 1960, expansion has averaged only 5.1 per cent per year and less than 4 per cent in the Seventies. Refining surpluses are becoming evident as growth in product demand declines due to slower economic activity, higher prices and the slow but steady effects of energy conservation. Expansion of refining capacity in the 1980s will be limited to three quite different requirements:

- Conventional refinery capacity at existing facilities may be expanded to meet local demands. Not much activity can be expected here.

23

- New capacity must be developed to refine heavy oils. Two types of heavy oils will require refining. The first is naturally occurring heavy oil. In the past, this oil has had limited domestic markets unless refined at great expense and has generally been exported to the United States. It is a recent government position that this oil should remain in Canada as feedstock for domestic refining. There is also a present surplus of heavy fuel oil, residual from refinery distillation. These surplus "resids" could also be re-refined to products of greater value. Several existing refineries can be expected to develop this capacity with revamping costs of about $300 million each.
- A third new oil-refining requirement will be the construction of new facilities geared to new sources of supply. The proposed new Shell refinery in Edmonton, for example, is designed primarily to upgrade synthetic crude from the tar sands.

Natural gas is processed close to the source of supply or main transmission line. Not surprisingly, 90 per cent of processing occurs in Alberta, with the balance in British Columbia and the Northwest Territories. Raw natural gas is processed before distribution to market to remove the relatively high proportion of sulphur found in Canadian gas and also to separate several valuable hydrocarbon constituents (propane, butane, isobutane) for other markets.

TABLE 2-3

FACILITIES AND CAPACITY FOR CANADIAN OIL REFINERIES AND NATURAL GAS PROCESSING PLANTS, 1947 – 78

	Oil Refineries		Natural Gas Processing	
	Number	Capacity (m^3/day)	Number	Capacity (MMf^3/day)
1947	32	41,970	—	—
1950	31	56,440	5	271
1955	42	98,300	9	418
1960	44	150,160	60	1,944
1965	40	173,160	109	6,064
1970	42	272,910	145	10,460
1975	39	342,510	212	12,854
1978	38	364,320	253	16,456

Sources: Canadian Petroleum Association, *Statistical Handbook*, 1978; Department of Energy, Mines and Resources, Operators List, *Natural Gas Processing Plants in Canada.*

As shown in Table 2-3, gas-processing capacity has expanded very rapidly during the Sixties and Seventies to keep pace with gas discoveries and expanding markets. In fact, capacity growth rates averaged 14.4 per cent per year between 1960 and 1978 with close to a quadrupling of facilities. Activity in the 1980s will see firstly the continuation of incremental additions to existing gas plants or the construction of small plants as production from existing gas fields is increased, and secondly the construction of new plants, depending on the location of new discoveries that can be economically developed and transported to markets—the frontiers or East Coast offshore discoveries, in particular.

Canadian ability to supply equipment to refineries generally appears to be increasing. Equipment and materials requirements for new construction normally account for 40—45 per cent of expenditure with the same for labour and between 10 and 20 per cent for engineering. As so few refineries have actually been built in the last decade, conclusions on Canadian content for the industry are somewhat speculative, and with only one major refinery planned for the Eighties, new refineries are not a significant consideration. The general view, however, is that as Canadian manufacturers have matured over the past twenty years, so has their ability to supply the refining industry.

There is, for example, nothing exotic about the equipment groupings required for a major refinery. As shown in Table 2-4, piping, fittings

TABLE 2-4
REFINERY EQUIPMENT/MATERIALS BREAKDOWNS

Category	Proportion of Total Equipment Cost (%)	Readily Available in Canada
Piping, fitting, valves	24	yes
Heat exchangers	13	yes
Compressors, pumps	12	some
Electrical equipment	11	yes
Instrumentation	9	no
Furnaces	9	yes
Pressure vessels	8	some
Structural steel	3	yes
Buildings	2	yes
Boilers	1	yes
Miscellaneous (concrete)	8	yes

Source: Imperial Oil Limited, Corporate Planning Department.

and valves represent almost 25 per cent of all equipment costs. All are commonly available in Canada, with the exception of highly specialized valves and fittings or stainless steel piping. Similarly, if manganese or cobalt alloys are used, Canadian sources are unavailable. Some of the larger of the valves, although manufactured in Canada, may in fact have low Canadian content, as large castings are generally beyond the requirements of Canadian manufacturers and have to be specially imported. Corporate engineers at Shell and Texaco suggest that these specialized requirements represent only a small proportion compared to those easily procured from Canadian manufacturers.

Specific problems in Canadian equipment manufacturing do arise for about 30 per cent of the equipment categories:

- Compressors in the design specifications required are consistently mentioned as difficult to have manufactured in Canada. Few firms can do the work and those that can are often fully booked, making delivery dates unacceptable.
- A refinery may require thirty to forty different vessels, most of which can be easily fabricated in Canada. Of all these vessels however, several will be high-pressure reactor vessels, which at over 500 tons of steel each are beyond the capacity of not only Canadian firms but most American as well. Although few in number, they may account for as much as 50 per cent of all vessel expenditures.
- Instrumentation is unavailable from any Canadian manufacturer. Instrumentation systems are generally bought as a complete package, together with computer assistance. Although bought through Canadian distributors or subsidiaries, these systems are overwhelmingly manufactured abroad.

These exceptions notwithstanding, domestic firms are increasingly capable of manufacturing refining equipment. Although few major new refineries can be expected through to 1990, the equipment requirements for plant expansion or revamping for heavy oil refining remain essentially the same. Specifications for the latter may change slightly but the most significant differences are in the engineering requirements, not the equipment.

The Canadian engineering community has not played a significant role in developing the nation's refining capacity. Refineries, being large and very expensive, have traditionally been far beyond the capabilities of Canadian engineering firms, and the major engineering contracts have been awarded to non-Canadians. Several Canadian companies have, however, evolved expertise in this field as the oil industry generally supports Canadian firms—in all except the largest projects—but their position in relation to the anticipated $300–400 million contract awards for several heavy oil revamping programs remains uncertain. The general consensus, even in the engineering community itself, is that only a few of the largest Canadian firms would be capable of undertaking such projects.

Equipment requirements for gas processing are somewhat more difficult to categorize than for refineries owing to the variety of processes employed. Removal of the "wet" components and hydrogen sulphide can be accomplished in any one of half-a-dozen ways. Most plants are specifically designed to treat gas from particular fields. According to industry observers, however, the major equipment items common to most of the processes, such as gas compressors, pumps, heat exchangers, valves, fittings and piping, are customarily obtained almost exclusively from Canadian manufacturers.

As most gas plant expansions in the Eighties will be modest in size ($6–30 million) no problems with equipment manufacturing are expected, unless shop capacity is stretched as a result of the cumulative effects of other projects. Even for the few large plants that may be anticipated, Canadian sourcing should be adequate. The Taglu gas plant, should the Dempster lateral pipeline be approved to process Mackenzie Delta gas, will cost an estimated $1 billion, for example. Components would be predominantly Canadian, fabricated in 1,000-ton modules and barged to the site. Depending on the route chosen, fabrication could take place in Vancouver, Hay River or even Montreal.

As with refineries, the engineering for all but the smallest of the gas plants is performed by non-Canadian firms.

Although the oil and gas industry increasingly stresses Canadian participation, its history demonstrates a continuing desire to contract with experienced firms. Experience with the smaller jobs has incrementally improved the ability of Canadian firms to perform the design engineering required, but their competitive advantage for what few large jobs will be undertaken over the next decade will be confined to their national identification. In an attempt to break the traditional barriers of size and experience, many Canadian firms are contemplating the possible advantages of entering permanent joint ventures with larger, internationally oriented firms.

Pipeline Construction

Canada has a thirty-year history in pipeline construction linking the major oil and gas producing regions in Western Canada through to Montreal and to export markets in the United States. The crude oil pipeline system consists of two main trunk lines, one stretching 2,150

27

miles from Edmonton to Montreal and the Great Lakes region of the United States and the other, 723 miles from Edmonton to Vancouver and the northwestern United States. The natural gas pipeline system has three large domestic systems. The first is operated by Alberta Gas Trunk Line and collects gas from the field and delivers it to provincial boundary connections to other trunk lines. The longest transmission system is operated by TransCanada PipeLines: gas is received at the Alberta/Saskatchewan border and flows eastward to Winnipeg where the line branches, north over the Great Lakes to Toronto and Montreal, and south to United States markets. The third major system transports gas from fields in northeastern British Columbia to regional distributors in the province and exports to the United States. A final system is the short 107-mile section of pipe in Alberta that is the key link in the Alberta/California gas export system.

Total installed pipe mileage has grown by 17 per cent per year since 1950, although in the Seventies activity was mostly confined to looping existing lines and developing distribution systems because of a lack of major projects other than the Sarnia to Montreal link completed in 1976. As shown in Table 2-5, by the end of 1978 over 114,-000 miles of pipe had been installed.

TABLE 2-5
PIPELINE MILEAGE IN CANADA,
1950 – 78

| Year | Oil Pipelines | Natural Gas Pipelines | | | Total |
		Gathering	Transmission	Distribution	
1950	1,423	—	—	—	1,423
1955	5,079	4,582	—	5,683	15,344
1960	8,435	3,680	10,715	18,419	41,249
1965	12,315	5,206	14,206	24,661	56,388
1970	17,062	6,791	19,282	33,840	76,975
1975	19,799	9,635	25,962	41,410	96,806
1978	21,512	12,578	28,577	51,376	114,043

Average Annual Growth Rate (all lines)

1950 – 60	40.0%
1960 – 70	6.4%
1970 – 78	5.0%
1950 – 78	17.0%

Source: Statistics Canada, *Oil Pipeline Transportation,* Catalogue 55-201; Statistics Canada, *Gas Utilities,* Catalogue 57-205.

28

Over $4.7 billion in the past twenty years have been spent on pipelines in Canada, and the indications are that another $17.4 billion could be spent in the next decade. In addition to ongoing looping programs of existing lines and expansion of natural gas distribution and collection systems, several large projects will dominate the pipeline scene if final approval is forthcoming: for example, the Foothills Yukon natural gas pipeline will, because of its location, be built for costs of $12 billion, unmatched in pipeline history. By comparison, the modest Montreal/Quebec City/Maritimes link will cost $1.5 – 2 billion.

Canadian manufacturers have evolved a very high capability to supply the needs of the pipeline industry. Existing pipelines are in the order of 90 per cent Canadian in content, and virtually all sourcing of material is done through Canadian firms. Because pipelines are typically interprovincial in nature they come under the jurisdiction of the National Energy Board, which reviews all applications before licensing is provided. Canadian content is now one of many factors the board considers upon project application, with its significance increasing where competing projects are involved. As a result of NEB reviews of Canadian content, the pipeline industry is one of the few sectors which routinely demands information on direct and component imports.

At its simplest, constructing a pipeline is basically no less than laying a pipe in the ground and installing equipment to facilitate the flow of oil or gas through the length of the pipe. It is not surprising, therefore, that the construction and installation costs are generally by far the most significant component of project costs, with a lower proportion spent on equipment and materials. Recognizing that the proportion of project costs will vary from project to project, a typical breakdown (excluding financing) would approximate the following: construction/installation—50 per cent; equipment/materials—35 per cent; other (engineering, administration)—15 per cent. Of the equipment and materials actually consumed, the pipe itself is by far the most significant, often representing 50 per cent of total requirements and 20 per cent of project costs. Canadian pipe is high-strength, high-impact carbon steel, considered by the pipeline community to be as good, if not better, than any in the world. Canadian content for the pipe, supplied by the Canadian steel industry, has been estimated at between 90 and 92 per cent; the balance is for raw materials such as coal or manganese used in making the pipe or for some pipeline coating materials not available in Canada.

Canadian pipe producers have a technological edge against competing firms in the United States that should ensure that virtually all pipe for major projects over the next decade will be Canadian. Pipeline manufacturers in the United States are only just beginning to produce the thin-wall, high-strength pipe that has been used in Canada for a decade. As a result, competing bids by U.S. firms generally reflect the fact that they are on the low end of the "learning curve" for this technology. The only effective competition to Canadian firms is from Japan and Italy, although their advantage is considered to range from very slight to non-existent.

Equipment requirements, other than pipe, are also high in Canadian content and are generally easily sourced. Major equipment needs fall into three main categories: valves, fittings and compressor station requirements.

Valves required for pipelines run a full spectrum from the general purpose types to the large diameter specialty gate and ball valves used on the main trunk line. Most of these requirements can be met in Canada except for the very large forty-eight-inch gate and ball valves proposed for the Alaska Highway natural gas pipeline. There are indications, however, that several Canadian firms have recognized these large valves as a useful addition to their manufacturing mix and are considering rounding out their production to provide a full range of valves. Limited domestic markets for valves over thirty inches, however, will necessitate some reliance on export markets for production to remain viable.

Pipe fittings cover a range of products, including flanges, headers, elbows, reducers and a variety of others. Manufacturing capacity is considered to be adequate in supplying most needs, although again because of a limited domestic market for large-diameter fittings in the past, not all requirements are likely to be met. The majority will be, however, as imports are estimated to be in the range of 15 – 20 per cent, principally in the form of low-priced items from Japan. This is an area where an import substitution program may prove useful.

Compressor station equipment incorporates the most advanced technology used for a pipeline. Although there are many Canadian firms in this area, virtually all are subsidiaries of international firms. As such their component sourcing programs may not always be geared to other Canadian firms. Many, however, have negotiated international marketing rights for their equipment and have strong export market development programs. Overall, Canadian content would appear to be in the 70 – 75 per cent range for special items such as jet or industrial gas turbines and generator sets—the most important components of compression equipment. The exact content will depend on which of the subsidiary firms are selected. Several companies are developing world-class Canadian-designed-and-produced industrial gas turbines; others rely essentially on parent-developed technology.

30

Imported equipment generally reflects specialty products that are uneconomical to produce in Canada at the moment. Industry observers have suggested these costs are very small in relation to total project costs, probably in the order of 2 per cent. The most important import requirements are for:

- specialty and large-diameter valves;
- special fittings;
- turbine rotors and blades;
- gas turbines for refrigeration;
- most instrumentation equipment.

The laudable level of Canadian content achieved by pipeline constructors is somewhat tarnished by their use of imported construction equipment, however. While construction labour, engineering and management are entirely Canadian, in the order of 85 per cent of construction equipment is imported. Smaller equipment such as trucks, trailers and loaders are generally sourced with no difficulty, but larger vehicles are not produced in Canada. Included here are items such as pipelayers, bulldozers and side-boom tractors. Generally, Canadian-produced heavy construction equipment is unavailable to all Canadian projects. Equipment types are very diverse, are high in unit value and, therefore, are low-volume items for which domestic manufacturing has to date not been viable. Nevertheless, Canada is a major market for heavy construction equipment. Development of large-scale production of heavy equipment for domestic and export markets may over the next decade be a valuable contribution to the Canadian manufacturing base.

Electric Utility Capabilities

Canadian utilities should continue to show important, although compared to the previous twenty years somewhat modest, additions to capacity throughout the 1980s. As indicated in the previous chapter, the period from 1965 to 1978 witnessed close to a trebling of generating capacity, with capital expenditures representing 55 per cent of total private and public energy investment. On the basis of already committed projects, utilities in the Eighties should see an increase of a further 50 per cent in generating capacity and represent in the order of 30 to 40 per cent of the total energy investment mix.

The Eighties may very well be a transition period for the utilities. In addition to the generally downward revision in demand forecasts, three factors in particular indicate changing patterns:

- Large hydroelectric potential is currently confined to Quebec, Newfoundland, British Columbia and the Northwest Territories.

Expansion programs through the Eighties will use much of this currently untapped potential. Other provinces, such as Ontario, are assessing future small-scale hydro opportunities for peaking purposes.

- The nuclear program in Canada is at a standstill. Beyond the Ontario Darlington plant there are no new reactor orders.
- Expansion programs in provinces without additional hydro opportunities or interest in nuclear will see greater use of coal-fired conventional steam systems. An ever-increasing use of coal is likely both in the Eighties and Nineties.

Although the transition to coal may be increasingly evident, activity in the Eighties will be largely geared to clearing the order books for hydro and nuclear projects and their associated transmission facilities: areas in which Canadian manufacturers have generally proved their excellence.

Overall, Canadian manufacturing content is quite high, although the significance of equipment costs to total project expenditures varies widely. As indicated in Table 2-6, equipment requirements range from a low of 25 per cent for large hydro projects to 50 per cent of project costs for conventional thermal plants and transmission stations. Generally, the variation results from differences in the proportion of construction labour costs and, in the case of nuclear, from the relatively high cost of constructing heavy water facilities to supply the nuclear plant.

TABLE 2-6
REPRESENTATIVE BREAKDOWN OF
UTILITY PROJECT EXPENDITURES

	Construction	Engineering	Equipment	Other*
Hydroelectric	68	7	25	—
Steam				
Conventional	37	7	50	6
Nuclear power station	20	7	37	36**
Transmission lines	33	12	37	18
Transmission stations	20	15	50	15

* Other includes commissioning costs, overheads and project administration.

** 31% of project costs for a nuclear power station result from providing heavy water to the facility; roughly 60% of the cost for a heavy water plant is for equipment. Total nuclear equipment is therefore roughly 60%.

Canadian content is generally high for all aspects of the utilities programs. All construction and engineering, for example, is performed entirely by Canadian firms, professionals and manpower. As for equipment, the capacity of Canadian manufacturers to supply the diverse requirements of the utility sector is steadily improving and, in many cases, appears to have reached a practical maximum. Most major and minor equipment requirements are now *capable* of being sourced through Canadian manufacturers. As an indication of the high Canadian content achieved, the two largest utilities, Ontario Hydro and Hydro Quebec, reported 80 per cent and 89 per cent respectively for total purchases in 1978.

The high proportion of construction costs for major hydroelectric projects reflects the fact that these are basically civil projects. The largest cost component is related to building the immense reservoirs and dams, requiring an emphasis on field construction and management for excavation work and reinforcing steel and concrete. The situation is somewhat different for smaller projects used for peaking purposes. With reservoir building minimized, the relative significance of construction declines to roughly 45 per cent of expenditures, with equipment and materials increasing to about the same level.

There appear to be few problems in manufacturing equipment for hydro projects within Canada. The long Canadian history in hydroelectric development has resulted in many domestic firms gaining an international reputation for major requirements. Hydraulic turbine generator sets, for example, represent the largest single expense (up to 25 per cent of equipment costs), and several Canadian firms are among the world's best. The balance of equipment and materials used are standard electrical products, structural steel, and custom-made vessels that are not generally unique to a single manufacturer's experience and are readily sourced. The only common exceptions are monitoring equipment and construction equipment:

- Monitoring and instrumentation equipment is generally unavailable from any Canadian manufacturer, although it can be bought through Canadian distributors.
- Construction equipment is 90 per cent supplied from the United States or Europe, generally on consignment to construction contractors from large dealers or directly from the manufacturers. Large off-highway trucks, loaders and bulldozers, in particular, are common to hydroelectric projects.

A more discouraging note for hydro-oriented manufacturers is the distinction between their capacity to supply domestic projects and instances where they have not been price competitive against foreign bidders. Many utilities across the country operate under a lowest-cost bid evaluation, with international competition. Although specific Canadian manufacturers are generally internationally competitive, many foreign firms enjoy the support of home governments offering guaranteed prices or financing arrangements against which unsupported domestic firms may not be able to compete. Several examples of alleged marginal pricing or concessional financing guarantees have been noted by industry observers, particularly in British Columbia and Manitoba. This topic will be discussed again in a wider context in Chapter 3.

With few exceptions, the ability of Canadian firms to supply conventional steam generating facilities is also quite high: the major exception being thermal turbine generator sets. Excluding the turbine generators, Canadian content can be in the order of 90 per cent, including them, about 70 to 75 per cent.

Thermal markets in Canada have developed much more slowly than in the United States and Europe as a result of the huge potential offered by domestic hydro resources. Consequently, many foreign generating markets matured with a greater emphasis on thermal generating equipment, the most significant of which is the turbine generator. To date the huge capital investment required, in facilities and technology, and a limited domestic market have precluded Canadian manufacturers entering into this market, which is already dominated by a handful of international firms. Global overcapacity in production facilities should also ensure that Canadian manufacturers will not enter the turbine generator market at least during the next decade.

The balance of major equipment requirements includes such items as piping, valves, fittings, pumps, boilers and heat exchangers, all of which are readily available from Canadian manufacturers. Although these are generally available, international competition for the thermal markets is strong, and as with hydro, there is no guarantee that orders will in fact be placed in Canada. In addition, the final Canadian content of many items will often depend on which domestic manufacturer receives the order, since most are subsidiaries of international firms with quite different sourcing programs for components.

The remaining exceptions to domestic manufacturing capability are for specially designed or high-technology items with which Canadian firms have either limited experience or limited domestic market opportunities. Specialty valves, pumps and fittings are most often mentioned, as are the instrumentation equipment and control panels. In relation to total project costs, these items generally represent only nominal expenditures.

There is little reason why virtually 100 per cent of equipment sourcing for transmission lines and transformer stations cannot be manufactured by Canadian firms. For the lines, roughly 75 per cent of equipment expenditures are for structural steel and conducting wire, and the balance for concrete and reinforcing steel. So long as lead times are respected, few problems should be encountered. Equipment requirements for the transformer station are generally more sophisticated but just as easily bought through Canadian manufacturers. Transformers, relays and switching gear make up 60 per cent of equipment requirements, and with the exception of some new European technology in switch gear (only used in high-density urban environments), all requirements are supplied through domestic firms. The balance of station expenditures is for structural steel, concrete, wiring and miscellaneous items.

Nuclear Power
The Canadian nuclear industry is possibly the best current example of Canadian manufacturers successfully entering and supplying the needs of a high-technology energy sector. About one hundred manufacturing firms are committed in various degrees to supplying the nuclear steam supply system for nuclear power plants. Their direct employment is estimated at 6,000. The nuclear industry is also an example of the potentially disastrous effects of production facilities expanding to meet forecast equipment requirements that then fail to materialize.

The CANDU nuclear system is uniquely Canadian in concept, design and execution. Not surprisingly, the industry has been structured to emphasize Canadian participation and today represents a blend of efforts involving government, electric utilities and private industry. A representative structuring of the industry is shown in Table 2-7.

From design through construction of a nuclear power facility, Canadian content averages 90 per cent, with equipment as the largest cost component. Two facilities are in fact required, the nuclear power station (NPS) and the heavy water plant (HWP), which supplies the main station with the heavy water required by the CANDU technology. On average the two facilities achieve 90 and 88 per cent Canadian content respectively.[3] For the NPS, 37 per cent of total cost is for equipment and 31 per cent for heavy water. For the HWP, 64 per cent of the investment is in equipment.

All construction and design engineering is performed by Canadian firms, or personnel employed by Atomic Energy of Canada Limited (AECL) or by the utilities.

Close cooperation between the manufacturers, the utilities and AECL has encouraged the manufacturing community to supply the vast majority of equipment requirements for the CANDU system: roughly 75 – 85 per cent for both the NPS and HWP. In addition, the

TABLE 2-7
STRUCTURE OF THE CANADIAN
NUCLEAR INDUSTRY

Mining and Refining:	There are six active uranium mining and associated milling operations in Canada, four located in Ontario and two in Saskatchewan. Eldorado Nuclear Limited, a Crown corporation, operates the only uranium refinery in Canada, located at Port Hope, Ontario. A second refinery is proposed by Eldorado to be located at Blind River in northwestern Ontario and a third to be located in Saskatchewan. Historically, 90% of Canadian-produced uranium has been exported.
Research and Development:	Virtually all R and D work is performed by the Atomic Energy of Canada Limited (AECL), funded primarily by the federal government. A porportionately much smaller amount is conducted by universities, the utilities and manufacturing companies.
Engineering and Design:	The AECL has been responsible for all nuclear engineering on export reactors and most domestic stations to date. Ontario Hydro continues to develop its capability with the aim of ultimately undertaking most of its work internally. Private engineering and consulting firms are involved in linking the "nuclear steam supply system" to the generating part of the plant.
Manufacturing:	Private manufacturing companies are involved in providing equipment and structural materials. Of 100 principal companies, roughly a third can be regarded as having a major commitment to the industry (on the basis of total company sales). Manufacturing activity is concentrated almost entirely in Ontario.
Construction:	Overall project management generally is the responsibility of the utilities. The bulk of construction is carried out by both the utilities and construction/contractor companies.
Operations and Maintenance:	All procurement and operating decisions are conducted by the utilities.

industry, through AECL and Ontario Hydro procurement programs, has developed at least two Canadian suppliers for major components, thus encouraging price competition, for example, for the calandria vessel (which houses the reaction process) and for the processing of fuel bundles. Maintaining price competition is considered essential to ensure cost effectiveness and technical innovation throughout the industry.

Equipment required for the nuclear power station can be broken down into two components: the nuclear steam supply system, representing half of the equipment costs; and the balance of the plant, including the power generation system representing the other half.

The nuclear steam supply system (NSSS) is the heart of the technical innovation that Canadian manufacturers must be capable of meeting. Specifications are demanding and the margin for error is minute. Much of the equipment for this system is custom manufactured and some items require lead times as long as six years. The following are the major equipment items with estimates of requirements likely to be manufactured by Canadian firms: fuel-handling system—100 per cent; steam generators—100 per cent; calandria shell—100 per cent; steam generator tubing—75 per cent; heat transfer pumps—100 per cent; condensors and tubing—100 per cent; switch gear—70 per cent.

The balance of the CANDU nuclear power station is a marriage of conventional thermal equipment to the specially designed NSSS. Turbine generators are the most important part of the power generating system and the most expensive, representing in the order of 15 per cent of all equipment costs. These turbine generators are essentially the same as those used for a conventional thermal system, although somewhat larger and operate at slower speeds. The same problems of sourcing this equipment is evident, however, and turbine generator sets typically average no more than 25 to 40 per cent in Canadian content. Even this content is due to agreements with the supplier to assemble some components in Canada. The balance of the plant equipment is common to most power generation systems: transformers, switch yard equipment and materials-handling items. All are generally capable of being manufactured in Canada.

There are several high-technology areas where imports have been required, however, and although Canadian content has been generally increasing over the past few years, further import substitution is not likely in the near future. According to senior officials at Ontario Hydro, a combination of tight and uncertain domestic markets and poor export performance has resulted in little incentive for companies to engage in further investment for some high-technology, low-production-run items. Combined with cuts in expenditure programs of the major utilities, further investment is unlikely. The following includes the most significant of these areas:

- Turbine generators, already discussed.
- Seamless alloy tubing is not available on a commercial scale in Canada. A new facility at Arnprior, Ontario, has not found a market large enough to match the production potential or economies of scale of foreign firms. A few international firms dominate the world market.
- Stainless steel plate, castings and tubing are unavailable in Canada.
- Roughly 20 per cent of specialty valves (either in design or by type alloy) must be imported.
- Specialty switch gear from Europe incorporates technology unmatched anywhere in the world.
- Instrumentation and computer equipment is imported from Europe and the United States.

Although generally not significant individually, except for the turbine generators (which alone may be 10 – 15 per cent of equipment costs), cumulatively these specialty items can account for up to 25 per cent of the equipment costs for the nuclear power station.

Overall, however, Canadian manufacturers have responded very well to the equipment demands of the nuclear industry. It seems, however, that many in the nuclear manufacturing community have responded too well. Within the nuclear and manufacturing communities alike, there is a growing concern about the effects of a substantially reduced nuclear program in Canada. According to a senior planning official at Ontario Hydro, "The greatest challenge is not increasing Canadian content but how to keep the industry viable through the coming lean period."

The manufacturing community dedicated to the nuclear industry is currently characterized by severe underutilization of installed capacity. The Leonard report, cited earlier (see note 3 for this chapter), suggests an average utilization of 50 per cent of capacity in 1977/78, a year of peak activity with manufacturing of equipment items for seven NPS and three HWP. These estimates are averages where there are two (or more) manufacturers. Often one may be fully booked while another has almost no work. Even in the case of some single supply sources, utilization is in the region of 50 per cent. Although it is difficult to generalize, the majority of companies require two to three reactor orders per year to fully utilize their work force and facilities; few can remain viable where volume falls to less than one per year.

The reasons for such overcapacity are straightforward. As in other capital-intensive industries characterized by supply equipment requiring long manufacturing lead times (three to four years for the calandria shell, five to six years for steam generators), demand forecasts and market expectations govern investment decisions. Forecasts made in the mid-1970s for reactor orders have proven to be far too optimistic. Some examples:

- In 1974 the Department of Industry, Trade and Commerce projected an average of six orders per year from 1976 onwards.[4]
- In 1975 the Canadian Nuclear Association (CNA) forecast twenty-five domestic reactor orders between 1976 and 1980. In fact, there were six.[5]
- Again in 1975 the CNA forecast an equipment expenditure (in 1973 dollars) between 1980 and 1990 of $5.7 billion, trebling by the year 2000.[6]

Investment decisions were predicated on these forecasts. Both domestic and export markets have failed to materialize, however. In the domestic market, electric power forecasts are progressively falling, and potential order dates continually recede. The nuclear future in the principal market of Ontario is unclear with the order books, post-Darlington, empty. The recently released Porter Commission report advises the Ontario government that Ontario's requirements will be insufficient to ensure an order level of one reactor per year; indeed estimates by the commission suggest only one additional four-reactor 3,400-megawatt plant to be necessary through to the year 2000, and the report cautions that even this may be optimistic. The commission concludes that "if the industry wishes to survive, it must begin to search for opportunities to diversify."[7] Hydro-rich Quebec is stepping back from the nuclear option. Of the three reactors for the Gentilly power station, the first has been shut down since 1977, the second, under construction since 1973, will be on stream in 1981, and the third is not being seriously considered for the immediate future. The only other province to develop a nuclear capacity has been New Brunswick, with the 600-megawatt Point LePreau station. Expansion plans for a second unit are indefinite. As a result, manufacturing work-loads continue to fall and unless new orders are received, there will be no manufacturing work at all by about 1988.

The export market has also failed to materialize as expected. Competition has proved to be stiff for reactor sales and has been intensified by international revisions to demand forecasts. The effectiveness of Atomic Energy of Canada Limited as a marketing organization has also been questioned.

Consequently, the immediate future for the nuclear manufacturing community is not promising. The effects are beginning to be felt in the consulting engineering sector, which is the leading edge of the downturn. The 1979 *Statistical Profile* published by the Canadian Nuclear Association indicates a 15 per cent drop in employment for the consulting sector over 1978, compounding sharp declines over the previous three years. The manufacturing companies involved in the industry can be divided into two equally sized groups, half of which are at risk:[8]

- The first group has less than 20 per cent of its business in the nuclear field and is therefore relatively insensitive to nuclear work-load.
- The second group has from 20 to 100 per cent commitment. The investment in specialized skills and facilities makes it difficult or impossible to divert efforts into other fields. Casualties among this group are expected to be high.

Should the situation persist, it is highly unlikely that the two-supplier policies fostered by AECL and Ontario Hydro will survive. Should rationalization occur, leaving only one domestic manufacturer to fulfill any future medium-term orders, domestic price competition will be non-existent. Ontario Hydro procurement policy at that point would likely require foreign firms to be entered on the bidding list.

Emerging Energy Sources

Of the $210 billion anticipated to be invested in the various energy sectors, roughly 37 per cent will be spent on energy supply programs that are relatively new to the Canadian experience and, in many cases, new to the global experience. Oil sands, heavy oil, and frontier oil and gas exploration and development in hostile environments are cases in point in which Canadian enterprises are in the forefront of global activity. These areas require an advanced and evolving technology to overcome technical limitations to their exploitation. Manufacturing opportunities will be defined over the next decade by the extent and speed with which these technical limitations are overcome and by the resolve that energy proponents bring to exploiting the resource. This in turn relies on the economic and political environment within which these investments must take place. The response of Canadian manufacturers to these new opportunities will undoubtedly be conditioned by the prospects of continuing work, not just in the Eighties but in the Nineties and beyond.

Bitumen deposits of the oil sands type are located in a number of countries, most notably in Venezuela and the Soviet Union, but none are as large as the estimated 800 billion barrels of oil in place in the Athabasca region of Alberta. The challenge of the oil sands is first to recover the resource, which is more solid than liquid, and second to process it into a product suitable for further refining. Two plants in Alberta can boast the distinction of being the only commercial facilities in the world yielding a "synthetic" crude. The first, the Great Canadian Oil Sands (GCOS), was commissioned in 1967 after decades of pioneering work and millions of dollars of expenditures in development research. A second and larger plant than GCOS is the Syncrude operation which came on stream in 1978. Both use strip-mining techniques, scooping oil sands buried under shallow overburden to conveyors for processing. A new generation of larger facilities has been proposed for the Eighties, with investment in the order of $22 billion. Two of these are awaiting regulatory approval and federal/provincial oil-pricing agreements: Alsands is a strip-mining operation similar to the existing plants; and Cold Lake mobilizes a large deposit of very heavy oil (which is, however, lighter than Athabasca bitumen) by injecting steam into it through deep wells, permitting it to be pumped to the surface. Another mining plant, sponsored by Petro-Canada and Alberta Gas Trunk Line, is in the preliminary planning stages, and at least two others are at the conceptual stage of planning. Although some practical operating and design experience is now available as a result of GCOS and Syncrude, the industry is still very much on the lower end of the learning curve for these resources. There quickly arises the fundamental issue of who will, firstly, develop and effectively control the technology and, secondly, supply the equipment for a resource that, by 1990, may be producing as much oil as from conventional land-based oil reserves. Both existing operations have been severely criticized on these two performance criteria; technological credit and equipment sourcing are seen as being predominantly non-domestic. Syncrude, in particular, has been criticized for its low Canadian content. Yet contrary to popular belief Syncrude did exhibit a high overall Canadian content, although not in the most critical areas. Of the $1.9 billion invested by Syncrude, an average of 80 per cent was *purchased* in Canada and 60 per cent in Alberta:[9]

- All construction subcontracts, manual and non-manual labour, for example, were entirely Canadian and together amounted to 46 per cent of total project costs.
- Project engineering and administration, although a smaller proportion at 8 per cent of costs, fared somewhat poorer with 43 per cent conducted outside Canada.
- Materials purchases represented 40 per cent of project costs with

60 per cent, by Syncrude estimates, sourced in Canada. This estimate is unquestionably high owing to the loose definition of Canadian content used by Syncrude. For this project, any supplier having a Canadian office was defined as Canadian: no distinction was made between distributors or manufacturers.

The prime engineering contractor, Bechtel of Canada, received criticism for the amount of project engineering performed outside Canada. Although roughly 60 per cent of engineering was performed by Canadians as subcontractors or through Bechtel's Calgary office, full engineering credit has been extended to Bechtel as the project manager. Bechtel had been, however, the contractor on the Great Canadian Oil Sands, and it is difficult to argue that their experience in pioneering the design engineering for this kind of technology would not have been an invaluable asset to the Syncrude operation. The fact that Bechtel gets full credit for the job is a quirk of the tough international engineering market, which tends to award more points for successfully managing a large job than for design engineering and equipment specification. On this last point it is generally acknowledged, even within the engineering community, that at the time there was no Canadian firm capable of performing the same role as Bechtel successfully accomplished. The manpower and financial resources were far beyond the capacity of even the largest Canadian engineering firm. Furthermore, the expertise of Canadian firms has tended to concentrate on engineering specialization with somewhat less attention paid to overall project management. The latter, as demonstrated in other sections, is typically performed by the utility or pipeline company client. Oil companies, however, have a strong preference for contracting one firm to be responsible for all aspects of a job, engineering, procurement of supplies, construction and, most importantly, overall project management. This fully integrated capacity for large projects is not available from domestic engineering firms even now.

Syncrude's ratio of 40 per cent imported equipment has been considered by many, particularly in Ontario, to be excessive, although no one has attempted to specify what it ought to have been. As a leading-edge type of project it is unlikely that the procurement system at Syncrude was geared to maximizing Canadian participation, even though this was a stated goal for the project. Recognizing the scale of development (over 250,000 different components), many procurement decisions could arguably have been made on the basis of convenience: the straightforward purchase of a well-known product as opposed to a time-consuming search for Canadian components that would require extensive engineering evaluation. In addition, with a large share of engineering design performed by non-Canadian engineers, it is not surprising that Canadian manufacturing capabilities were not readily recognized or used.

Future projects are being planned to alleviate many of these deficiencies. Lessons learned from Syncrude and GCOS—plus the legitimate opinion that most of the benefits from tar sands and heavy oil development should flow to local and other Canadian firms—have prompted project planners at Alsands and Cold Lake to more effectively match their requirements to Canadian capabilities.

Engineering and project management for both projects will be performed by formal joint ventures composed of a Canadian firm plus an overall project coordinator of some international stature. The size and distinctive expertise required by both these projects will allow each participant to perform all EPC- (engineering, procurement, construction) related functions within several different sections of the project. Such an arrangement will be a definite advantage for the successful Canadian firms. It will allow international recognition for both the design and management of individual work programs and credit for formal participation and risk sharing in the overall project. With more Canadians and Canadian firms playing an increasingly responsible role and gaining the critical "management" experience, the goal of Canadian firms taking the lead role in succeeding projects begins to become more realistic. The result will be more secure domestic control over the technology and a greater understanding of, and dialogue with, Canadian manufacturers. Both the technology and equipment will be exportable to other countries and projects. (More will be said on ensuring major project capability in the next chapter.)

Just as important is the realization that planning can increase the ability of the projects to use Canadian equipment and materials. The result should see in the order of 75 – 80 per cent of equipment requirements for Alsands, Cold Lake and succeeding projects being sourced through Canadian manufacturers. Oil sands and heavy oil plants can be broken down into three distinct components, each of which has a measure of Canadian manufacturing experience, namely:

- extraction of the oil, either through mining or wells;
- utilities, to provide process heat and power to the facilities;
- refining, to upgrade the oil into a transportable and marketable commodity.

The extraction technology is the most essential difference between *in situ* heavy oil development (Cold Lake) and oil sands mining (Alsands) and will yield the greatest variation in the ability to supply equipment. The mining and materials-handling equipment required by Alsands has traditionally been sourced outside of Canada and represents half of the major equipment requirements and 20 per cent of all equipment and materials expenditure. Major equipment includes reclaimers, draglines, stackers, cable reel cars and conveyors which are not available in Canada, although some assembly of structural components is performed in Alberta. Alsands will spend over $330 million for this equipment, 75 per cent from foreign sources. In contrast, the *in situ* process requires equipment more generally used in the petroleum industry (rigs and piping for example), 80 per cent of which can be easily supplied by domestic firms, as indicated in previous sections.

Utilities in the form of process steam and electricity will be required from on-site facilities. Since these will be conventional steam systems, equipment requirements will be similar to those required by provincial utilities, although more piping may be needed. Turbines and generators will be the main import requirements for both projects.

The upgrading plants will be somewhat different from conventional refineries because of the heaviness of the feedstock. Little information on the design of equipment to be used is available, but lack of domestic experience in heavy oil refining compared to the United States suggests imports may be quite high.

Needless to say, the volume of equipment required for these megaprojects is staggering. A partial list of the type and number required is shown in Table 2-8, compiled from preliminary information supplied by Alsands and Cold Lake. To ensure that Canadian firms are given the opportunity to supply the maximum amounts possible, several procurement decisions have been made to improve upon Syncrude practices:

- Domestic equipment suppliers and their capabilities are to be thoroughly researched through Canadian content managers working with the procurement offices.
- Tenders are to be awarded in small enough packages to allow the participation of smaller firms.
- Specifications are to be made consistent with products already manufactured in Canada, wherever possible.
- Project sponsors are to maintain communications with manufacturers through project specifications lists and conferences across the country.

In spite of these efforts to maximize Canadian content, some imports will be inevitable in addition to the major items already mentioned. They are strikingly similar to those mentioned for other energy sectors

TABLE 2-8
PARTIAL EQUIPMENT AND MATERIALS LIST
FOR ALSANDS AND COLD LAKE

Item	Number Required Alsands	Cold Lake
Drilling rigs	—	15
Draglines	4	1
Towers	*	435
Vessels	410	160
Heat exchangers	300	300
Crushers	2	1
Boilers	5	5
Pumps	1,000	1,200
Compressors	160	126
Valves	*	70,000
Turbine/Generators	7	6
Electric motors	800	1,000
Transformers	50	8
Concrete	230,000 m³	*
Piping	1,000,000 m	*
Steel	45,000 tonnes	*
Wire and cable	3,000,000 m	*

* Information unavailable.

and include special pumps, valves and fittings, alloy pipes and plating, instrumentation and control panels.

Procuring equipment from Canadian sources is not considered to be as big a problem as ensuring the availability of labour. The Cold Lake and Alsands projects alone will have peak manpower requirements of 8,300 and 10,200 employees respectively, across ten trades and several professions. Several studies[10] by project proponents and the Alberta government have indicated specific manpower shortfalls for several trades, given the base Alberta demand, maximum oil sands development (Alsands, Cold Lake, one other, plus two upgrading), several petrochemical facilities, the Foothills pipeline and other relatively minor projects coming on stream in the 1980s. Shortfalls are expected for pipefitters, boilermakers, steel fabricators, millwrights, operating engineers and pressure welders. Estimates indicate that labour supply for most of these trades will be in surplus for Canada as a whole but will be tight in Alberta even under an expanded apprenticeship program and with active recruiting programs throughout Canada. In two cases, pressure welders and millwrights, the available Canadian surplus will be inadequate to meet Alberta demands, and foreign recruiting is being considered.

Frontier and Offshore Exploration

Vigorous exploration and development of offshore and frontier resource areas are an unquestioned requirement if Canada is to match oil demand with domestic supply by 1990 (see Chart 2-1). The most recent discoveries along the East Coast have given some measure of credibility to the attainment of such a goal. The true scope of the opportunity is, however, still clouded by uncertainty: physical oil reserves are unproven, the technology of production from known fields is vague, and the economics of bringing the oil to the marketplace are uncertain. Nonetheless, the opportunity is sufficiently attractive to encourage an expected $48 billion investment program in these areas over the next decade.

Such a program dwarfs past experience in the offshore and frontier regions. For comparison, by 1978 the oil and gas industry had invested $2.8 billion in the Arctic islands and Northwest Territories since 1951 and only $646 million along the East Coast since 1967: 90 and 95 per cent respectively being invested since 1970.[11] Canada's experience is, therefore, somewhat limited compared to what lies ahead in the 1980s. With limited offshore exploration experience and no domestic field development and production experience, Canadian participation will be severely challenged by the experience of foreign firms.

Canadian capabilities are embryonic but increasingly available. Equipment such as drill ships, drilling derricks, manned and remotely controlled submersibles, seismic equipment and subsea surveying systems have been developed by Canadian firms. Ironically, firms in the evolving ocean industry have relied on international markets. As activity in Canadian waters accelerates, the development of Canadian industrial, technological and scientific capacity must be encouraged.

Given the uncertainty that surrounds this area, forecasting Canadian content is obviously premature, but an indication of the likely directions required as a precondition for high involvement and of gaps in Canadian capabilities[12] will give some perspective of the manufacturing opportunities.

The predominant expense in the exploratory phase is for the drilling rig. Three types of rigs are used in Canadian waters:

- A floating drill ship that has a derrick amidship and a drill hole in the centre of the hull is the type of system used in the High Arctic and off Labrador.

46

CHART 2-1
OIL SUPPLY AND DEMAND ESTIMATES,
1978 – 90

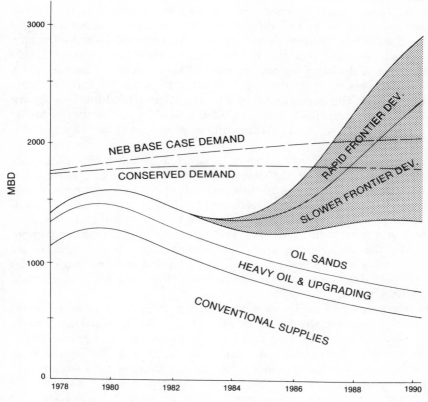

Source: Canadian Petroleum Association, *Position Paper Regarding Canada's Oil Policy Options,* 1979.

- The semi-submersible rig, which is more typical of offshore drilling practice along the East Coast, is a large platform resting on the surface with a deep substructure to minimize movement.
- The jack-up rig is a platform supported by three to four legs jacked down to the sea bottom. These rigs are only used in depths of 200 feet or less.

Both the semi-subs and jack-ups are expensive to build (over $35 million) and to operate ($100,000 a day including labour). Drilling just one well, according to company officials, can cost as much as $10 million in the High Arctic, $15 million at Hibernia on the East Coast, and $35 million in the Beaufort sea. In contrast, land-based rigs generally cost $25,000 a day and $6 million to complete an average deep well.

Rigs are normally owned and operated by international contractors and hired out to the oil and gas industry wherever offshore drilling is required. There are few Canadian firms active in offshore contracting. Payouts on these rigs are not made until after five years of steady work; with drilling programs in most offshore locations limited to six months, work must be developed in other locations for the remainder of the year. The uncertainties of entering international markets against established competition have inhibited Canadian contractors in taking a lead role. Given more secure drilling programs in the Eighties, this will likely change.

Fabricating these rigs could be conducted in half-a-dozen locations along the East and West Coasts. Davies Shipbuilding in Quebec is the only active builder of semi-subs and jack-ups at the moment. Canadian content for these rigs is similar (70 – 80 per cent) to that of land-based rigs. They are essentially no more than a land rig supported by legs or a substructure. As with land rigs, the major equipment components, the draw-works, mud pumps and large diesel engines, are imported. Ensuring that fabrication is performed in Canada is essential if future design and technology improvements are to be performed within Canada.

The balance of exploration costs (in the order of 35 to 40 per cent) comes from such diverse areas as seismic surveys, helicopter rentals, consumable materials used in drilling (theoretically 100 per cent Canadian, except for some drill bits), work boats and the provision of offshore services such as drill stem testing, cementing contractors and catering services. All of these activities (except the manufacturing of helicopters) are generally considered to be already established and expanding rapidly.

Future drilling requirements are expected to stretch existing technology to the limit. Current programs are restricted to a brief summer season. The next generation of drilling programs will attempt to extend this season, and will venture into much deeper and hostile ice-infested environments. Future requirements, then, will place Canadian firms in an ideal position to develop platforms compatible with moving ice environments, to improve drilling techniques and to extend drilling capacity to deeper water. With the international trend toward deep water drilling, Canadians may quickly find themselves faced with an opportunity at the leading edge of an exportable technology.

Although they are high, offshore exploration costs are dwarfed by development costs, which, according to oil industry representatives, are likely to be as much as six times more expensive than exploration. In contrast, the experience of land-based development in Alberta has shown the exploration costs to be double the development costs. Since Canada has no practical domestic experience in frontier and offshore field development, its rapid entry into this activity will soon be urgent.

In the development phase following an initial discovery, further wells are drilled with exploratory rigs to delimit the field and prove production potential. If the field is found to be commercially viable, production equipment is brought to the site. Production platforms fixed to the ocean floor, such as those used in the North Sea by Britain and Norway, are the most prominant of the production systems used. Because of the North Sea experience, British and Norwegian firms are leaders in the design and fabrication of drilling and production platforms. Canada will be hard pressed to compete with their proven successes.

The North Sea and global expertise is, however, limited to production depths of 1,000 feet of water. As drilling programs find fields at depths greater than this, or as production systems are required in more hostile environments, Canada will again be in a position to develop novel technology. Man-made islands on the frontiers and floating platforms capable of evading ice flows along the East Coast will be examples of meeting the technical challenges that a unique Canadian environment poses. If the climate for innovation is right, there is little reason for Canadian firms not to develop the technology. With the drilling and production platforms costing an estimated 40 to 50 per cent of total development costs, developing indigenous technology and equipment supply capability is obviously desirable. To be sure, Canadian manufacturers already make a fairly extensive proportion of the equipment and materals required (Table 2-9), but developing and adapting new technology can ensure that work is performed within Canada, thus giving Canadian firms a more solid opportunity to participate.

The last stage in the development process is to transport the produced oil to shore. This can be done either by pipeline or tanker, depending on the size of the field, the topography of the ocean floor and of course the limits of pipeline technology and economics. As most offshore petroleum resources will require underwater pipelines for production, the development of Canadian expertise is exportable. The presence of ice packs in some future locations will require the development of techniques and equipment for pipelaying through ice and for subseabed burial of the pipe. Tanker transport will be a real possibility for initial discoveries if they are to move quickly to market.

49

TABLE 2-9
A PARTIAL LIST OF EQUIPMENT/MATERIAL
REQUIREMENTS FOR OFFSHORE PRODUCTION

Fixed wing aircraft and helicopters
Communication equipment
Compressors
Computer facilities
Drilling rigs
Electrical equipment
— power sources
— transmission equipment
— switch gear
Heating, air conditioning and ventilation systems
Hydraulic equipment
Instrumentation
Oil well drilling equipment
Oil well production equipment
Power transmission equipment
Pumps
Ships, boats, vessels
— supply boats, barges
— pipelaying barges
— submarine work boats
— tank ships
— tugs
Subsea equipment
Pipe
— drill pipe, casings
— line pipe
Valves
Wire Rope, winches, cables

Source: Pallister Resource Management Ltd., *Steering a Course to Excellence: A Study of the Canadian Offshore Oil and Gas Service Industries,* National Research Council of Canada, 1977.

In addition, most of the natural gas deposits so far discovered in the Arctic islands are so dispersed that serious attention is being given to transport of liquified natural gas by tanker to terminals along the East Coast. Most of this technology is already available in the international community but will require substantial design modifications for the Arctic environment, including the design and construction of the LNG ice-breaking tankers themselves.

The volume of tanker traffic in the North will ensure opportunities not only in vessel design and construction, but also in high-technology navigation systems. Dome Petroleum, for example, optimistically projects a requirement of ninety ships by 1990 to develop the Beaufort sea. For the efficient movement of this traffic, sophisticated electronic remote-sensing, navigation and ice detection systems will be needed. Their development offers significant domestic and export opportunities to the Canadian electronic industry.

In summary, many of the components for exploration and operating systems at sea are similar to those on land, where Canadians already have a high level of expertise. For the offshore, however, Canadian participation has been limited by the short history of active Canadian involvement in this area. The contrast is with other countries' service companies which have been engaged in providing offshore service for several decades and have evolved into an internationally mobile industry.

Although Canadian capabilities are already present in several areas and Canadian companies are already successfully engaged in export markets, these capabilities will have to be drastically extended if Canadians are to attain a good measure of technological control over their offshore resources.

While many firms are undoubtedly eager to provide many of the traditional services and develop new technology, the base from which they operate is limited compared to the reputation, size and financial resources of those they will be competing against. Thus a political and economic climate conducive to their participation will have to be developed.

$67 Billion in Equipment Required

It should be quite clear when discussing future expenditures for energy projects that only a proportion of the investment actually relates to materials and equipment. Of the major energy sectors discussed in the preceding sections, there is a large variation in these proportions: from a low of 25 per cent for large hydroelectric projects up to 60 per cent for nuclear facilities (including both the main station and the heavy water plant). When considering the mix of investment, which comprises the $210 billion investment program and the relative equipment requirements of the various projects, the opportunity to Canadian manufacturers will be in the order of $67 billion (Table 2-10). Past Canadian industrial performance suggests $48 billion could be sourced through Canadian manufacturers:

● Fairly reliable estimates can be developed for $40.8 billion in equipment and materials required for the utilities and the non-exploration and development functions of the oil and gas industry: refineries, pipelines and estimates for the tar sands. Based on past experience, 75 – 80 per cent of these equipment requirements could be sourced from Canadian manufacturers, representing $32 billion in orders.

- More speculative estimates for the non-project-related oil and gas expenditures both in producing regions and in the frontiers are required. For producing regions, the high degree to which work is contracted out makes it difficult to separate overheads, profits and labour from actual equipment costs. Assuming fabrication of fifty rigs per year and a high Canadian content for consumables and well head equipment, $8 billion would not be unreasonable. For the frontier area, uncertainties concerning the nature of equipment required and the degree of contracted work make any equipment forecasts highly speculative. Based on experience in the North Sea and industry rules of thumb, perhaps $8 billion could be for equipment sourced through Canadian firms. Given strong federal and provincial resolve to maximize Canadian content, the assumed 50 per cent penetration by Canadian firms could be understated. The Norwegian and British experience indicates a much higher penetration to be possible.

Several sectors, because of their relative insignificance in relation to total forecast investment and the modest scale of the projects involved, were not specifically assessed. Uranium and coal mining, for example, represent only 3 per cent of projected investment. Both have a long history of development in Canada, and both are considered areas where Canadian participation should be high, except for some specialized mining equipment. Alternative energy investments should also exhibit a high degree of Canadian content, both for the technology developed and for the equipment required—although it is recognized that global competition will be intense. A growing number of Canadian companies are involved in the renewable field, some at the forefront of global technical advances.

The $48 billion value of equipment to be ordered through Canadian firms is based on past experience in related projects and the subjective opinions of participants in the energy industry. As noted earlier in this chapter, there is some difficulty in determining what proportion of components for this equipment is in fact imported. The estimate is an indication of the manufacturing opportunity in Canada, based on the types of equipment that in the past have been readily available from Canadian firms rather than on a definitive statement on actual orders. Whether or not the ability will be actualized will depend on a number

TABLE 2-10
MANUFACTURING OPPORTUNITIES FROM
ENERGY INVESTMENTS, 1980 – 90

	Forecast Expenditures (in billions of 1980 $'s)	Historical Equipment Requirements		Estimated* Canadian Content	
		%	orders	%	orders
Reliable Estimates					
Utilities					
Conventional thermal	8.4	50	4.2	60	2.5
Hydroelectric	34.0	25	8.5	80	6.8
Nuclear	11.9	60	7.1	80	5.7
Transmission	9.0	45	4.1	90	3.6
Oil & gas related					
Refineries	5.0	44	2.2	60	1.3
Pipelines	17.4	35	6.1	90	5.5
Tar sands	21.4	40	8.6	75	6.6
Total	107.6	38	40.8	78	32.0
Speculative Estimates					
Oil & gas exploration & development					
Producing areas	42.0	24	10.1	80	8.1
Frontier/Offshore**	48.0	34	16.3	50	8.2
Total	90.0	29	26.4	65	16.3

* Value of orders to Canadian manufacturing firms.
** No reliable estimates on equipment orders are possible. The British experience during initial activity in the North Sea indicates 34% of expenditures related to equipment with 70% penetration by British companies. Assume Canadian firms could achieve 50% penetration.

of factors and limitations that can be observed throughout the energy industry. The more significant of these include:

● The incentive to expand production facilities. The shop capacity of many firms to supply equipment requirements has in the past not been a major problem, except during periods of peak activity. Undoubtedly some orders during these periods have been lost due to unacceptable delivery schedules. Expansion of shop capacity over the next decade will take place, but if the pace of expansion

53

is to match demand, clearer signals to manufacturers will have to be given on the project mix and continuity of investment programs.

- The type of equipment required is international in character. Competition from foreign suppliers can be high where bids are put to international tender. There is concern that marginal pricing and home government support for foreign firms often place Canadian firms at a disadvantage. An effective, national procurement policy is lacking in Canada.
- Canadian firms often lack the size, international stature and financial resources of their international competitors. This is especially the case for engineering firms, which for lack of size are often unable to participate in many large projects. The leading edge of technological advances is, as a result, frequently performed by non-Canadian firms.
- The equipment types show high variation in size, quality and specialization. Canadian manufacturers of such common equipment as valves and fittings often do not have a line of products complete enough to supply the entire energy sector. Some of the required products are of exotic materials and others have slight modifications in specifications. The ability to supply these products increases incrementally as demand and industry mature.

These issues, their significance and the approaches to their solution are discussed in the following chapter.

Issues and Approaches

3

The Canadian manufacturing community has for the most part done a creditable job in supplying the equipment and material requirements of the energy sector: many firms have in fact done remarkably well, considering the obstacles to be overcome. Its past performance for the utility and pipeline projects has shown that the manufacturing community can respond to quite diverse and exacting requirements. In areas such as the tar sands, refineries and drilling programs in the oil and gas industry, it has shown improvement over the past several years, and further improvement can be expected. Still other areas, such as the exploration and development programs in the Arctic frontiers and offshore along the East Coast, offer tremendous, though at present difficult to specify, opportunities.

That further opportunities are present in all these sectors is undeniable. To comment on the ways and means of capitalizing on the perceived opportunity to the fullest possible extent is a somewhat daunting task, given the breadth and depth of the energy industry; yet there are several common problems that can be addressed.

Solutions to these problems will come from a variety of sources: some as a result of government initiatives, others from industry. Several problems and suggested actions discussed in this chapter will deal with particular industry requirements, and others will deal with important preconditions to manufacturing involvement. Throughout, we can be guided by the rich experience Canadians already have in developing their energy resources. Being conscious of some key strategic lessons learned in the past can point to directions that should be followed to ensure the extended participation of Canadian industry.

There is little question that the greatest single barrier faced by manufacturers of energy-related machinery and equipment is the degree to which future domestic markets are uncertain. The ground rules under which future investment in the energy sector will occur are unclear, and lists of anticipated energy projects, their capital costs and timing are particularly short-lived. During the course of the writing and researching of this report, the ground rules for several sectors have in fact changed: the tar sands projects will no longer receive world oil prices for their products; the super depletion allowance for well drilling is not to be renewed; and federal/provincial negotiations on appropriate oil- and gas-pricing formulas are at a bitter deadlock. Add to this the confusion on future gas exports and the very uncertain role of nuclear energy in the future energy mix, and it can be seen that virtually every energy sector is in some way touched by a fundamental indecision in public policy. All of these problems will undoubtedly be resolved in one way or another, but the present piecemeal approach to planning virtually guarantees that others will arise. It is not hard to imagine the effects of this confusion at the conceptual stage on those responsible for production planning at the manufacturing level. Senior representatives of the Canadian Manufacturers Association are hearing such complaints with increasing frequency. Manufacturers are complaining that "the opportunities are real and exciting but project delays and uncertainty about future work programs make production forecasting virtually impossible."

The first step, and ultimately the most rewarding in actualizing these manufacturing opportunities, must be to remove these uncertainties. Without change here, any other action will result in little more than incremental improvement. Governments, energy proponents and industry must work together to remove the barriers:

- Governments must evolve an energy policy that clearly provides the ground rules for, and the preferred direction of, energy investments. Once formulated, it should be refined as needed but not drastically revised.
- Energy proponents must forecast their equipment requirements well in advance of tendering, and attempt to keep the manufacturing community informed of evolving conditions.
- Manufacturers and energy proponents must work and plan in concert to avoid bottlenecks and to ensure that the right product may be delivered at the right time.

A National Energy Development Plan

Industry observers are increasingly concerned about the year-to-year shifts in emphases by government programs from one energy activity to another. A senior representative of the Canadian Petroleum Association neatly summarizes this apparent preoccupation with finding the mother lode: "An energy strategy is absolutely critical to provide a sense of security to energy proponents and manufacturers alike. In the past, the oil and gas industry has witnessed too many flip-flops; with each new technology or promising field of activity the emphasis has shifted to the almost total exclusion of everything that came before. In the early Seventies we saw tremendous support for frontier development in the Mackenzie Delta. When discoveries failed to justify the huge expectations, attention shifted to the considerable potential of the tar sands and heavy oil deposits in Western Canada. Then came promising discoveries in the Arctic islands, followed by a reversion back to the tar sands investment plans of several companies. Today, the hope is that discoveries off the East Coast will make any other activity unnecessary."

It is the Canadian Petroleum Association's position that investment in all of these sources must be actively promoted if there is to be any chance of achieving self-sufficiency in the next decade. Although the association is admittedly in an advocacy position, these comments point to the need to evaluate a range of future energy supplies and to specify the proportion of the total energy mix they may take.

Given an energy policy, a national investment strategy or its equivalent must be evolved and designed to give clear signals to both energy proponents and manufacturers alike. The key here is not so much to develop long lists of projects as to identify project groupings with security of execution within established time frames. A common perception in the industry is the need for public authority to develop a timetable to bring resources on stream in a way that will create an orderly flow of capital, extend the life of non-renewable resources, and secure the likelihood of future orders for the manufacturing community. Given the need to expand manufacturing capabilities and the long lead times involved, forward planning by manufacturers must be made on the basis of prospects more than one or two projects down the road. If not, investment in plant capacity will be done on an incremental basis and reluctantly. The risk of idle capacity and manpower will guarantee minimum investment for minimum risk.

A sceptical manufacturing community must have some assurance that an investment timetable will not be too drastically altered during its execution. The severe overcapacity within the nuclear manufacturing industry, noted in the previous chapter, has occurred partly as a result of unfulfilled forecasts of future reactor sales. Additional casualties, if somewhat less well documented, are those manufacturers in Alberta and the rest of Canada who saw manufacturing opportunities for tar sands plants beyond Syncrude. Many manufacturers, according to a senior official in Alberta's Industrial Development Branch, invested in the perceived opportunity and got "burned" by the regulatory delays of both Alsands and Cold Lake. The delays continue as

Alberta and the federal government come to agreement on oil-pricing formulas.

A few experiences with idle capacity and the difficulties in holding staff over several years quickly lead to a sceptical industry. All sectors need a sense of continuity to plan effectively for the future; they need to be free from the "roller-coaster" effect of high activity to little or none.

An unfortunate fact of current investment in the energy industry is that supply of equipment and machinery is given provincial preference over national interest. Each province attempts to maximize the involvement of local firms and often offers incentives or "moral suasion" to encourage project proponents to consider the localization of supply as an additional and important factor in procurement decisions. Many firms feel compelled to trade economies of scale at a central plant for the increased prospect of receiving provincial contracts.

The Canadian manufacturing base, as a whole, is sufficiently mature to provide a very high proportion of equipment and machinery requirements to the energy industry. These requirements, however, are characterized by high product differentiation in both the type and size of equipment supplied. Given the wide variety and extensive product differentiation required by the energy industry and the generally limited domestic market for each type and size, the fragmentation of the Canadian market that can result through restrictive provincial purchasing policy and interprovincial competition should be viewed as a serious impediment to the expansion of production capacity. Regional development is obviously a legitimate concern for provincial governments, especially in the absence of a comprehensive national industrial strategy, but it should be approached with concern for the negative effects of fragmentation and overcapacity.

It is quite clear that there is no mutually shared procurement policy for Canadian products. The federal government must continue to make strong representations to the provinces and proponents of major projects, indicating the importance it places on a national sourcing program.

There are several indications that the importance of increasing Canadian content in energy projects has been recognized by federal and provincial governments. There have been various federal initiatives to study and monitor Canadian content in and industrial benefit from the development of Canada's natural resources. The Advisory Committee on Industrial Benefit from Natural Resources Development (ACIB) is an example of this. Established in 1975, this federal interdepartmental committee is comprised of representatives from four departments, and it monitors individual resource projects. Although the committee has

58

no executive authority, the departments represented do have authority for such areas as the provision of production leases, environmental impact statements and general regulatory control. Through moral suasion, the committee attempts to increase the sourcing of equipment in Canada, particularly in those areas exhibiting a substantial Canadian technology base.

Yet another federally sponsored initiative is the Task Force on Industrial and Regional Benefits from Major Canadian Projects. Senior representatives from business and labour have been drawn together to develop an inventory of major projects and make recommendations on how to increase the participation of the Canadian industrial base. Most government observers suggest this task force's recommendations will form the basis of future government policy. No unilateral federal government action is likely before the recommendations are made public towards the end of 1980.

However, some provisions to enhance Canadian content have been incorporated in recent legislation on specific projects. The strongest provision to date is in the Northern Pipeline Act administered by the Northern Pipeline Agency. Section 10 of the act states that "the company shall design a program for the procurement of all goods and services for the pipeline that ensures that:

i)   Canadians have a fair and competitive opportunity to participate in the supply of goods and services to the pipeline.
ii)   the level of Canadian content is maximized so far as practicable with respect to the origin of products, services and their constituent components.
iii) maximum advantage is taken of opportunities provided by the pipeline to establish and expand suppliers in Canada that can make a long-term contribution to the Canadian industrial base.
iv)   maximum advantage is taken of opportunities provided by the pipeline to foster research development and technological activities in Canada.

The first test of the act will be the Foothills prebuild pipeline. As will be seen later in the chapter, Foothills' procurement program has been strongly influenced by these Canadian content provisions.

A somewhat more difficult test of government resolve to increase Canadian content through the legislative stick is Bill C-20, the Oil and Gas Act, currently in the draft stage. It is hoped by many observers that this bill will contain Canadian content clauses at least as powerful as the Northern Pipeline Act. At issue is whether these clauses should be simply a policy statement or whether they should provide a strong legal framework for the monitoring and enforcement of Canadian content.

59

The provinces are also developing legislation to increase provincial content. Nova Scotia and Newfoundland in particular have introduced legislation that demands that Canadian and provincial firms be given a fair chance to compete. Unfortunately, the origin of this legislative resolve appears to have stemmed from the absence of prior federal mechanisms to achieve the same purpose.

The effectiveness of such government initiatives should not be underestimated. An indication of their effectiveness is the dominance of British and Norwegian firms participating in the North Sea development in each of their respective areas. Through quite different means, both have linked the granting of exploration and production acreage to industrial benefit.

The British approach requires operators to sign a "memorandum of understanding" specifying British content requirements. All purchases must be reported to the Offshores Supplies Office, and any order of more than $100,000 must be reported before ordering. In this way the office alerts British manufacturers to evolving opportunities, and is in a position to pressure companies to maximize British content. As a result, British content for North Sea activities has jumped from about 30 per cent to a recently reported 78 per cent.

The Norwegian approach, although different, has proved just as effective. Oil companies must propose what industrial benefit to Norway will result from a successful bid for acreage. Any future bid is evaluated against past performance. In addition, the government-owned oil company, Statoil, takes not only a significant equity position in any producing field but within five years from commencing operation also becomes the operator. Very effective leverage is provided with Statoil acting as a major participant in procurement decisions. By way of example, the Statfjord field is 45 per cent owned by Statoil and 15 per cent by Mobil, the current operator. Within five years, Statoil will become the operator, as well as retaining its equity position. In contrast, the Hibernia field off Newfoundland is controlled by Mobil with Petro-Canada, as the government agency, having only about 15 per cent equity. Participation at this level provides some information on how the project is developing but absolutely no leverage in the important procurement decisions for the project. These decisions are left to Mobil's head office in New York.

These foreign experiences have been introduced as examples of the effectiveness strong government resolve may have on the procurement of equipment and not as models for Canadian incentives. A more comprehensive strategy is required for the diversity of energy projects Canada will face over the next decade. In any event, Canada cannot use the leverage of acreage bids as in these offshore examples; industry observers suggest that the most promising frontier and offshore acreage has already been assigned.

"Buy Canadian" Procurement Policies

Procurement policies attempting to maximize Canadian content are not a novel concept and have been practised for several years, although with varying degrees of commitment and success. (See Appendix.)

Energy projects sponsored by provincial governments or regulated by provincial and federal governments are encouraged to maximize participation of provincial or national firms. Of the utilities, only Ontario Hydro specifically encourages Canadian participation regardless of manufacturing location. Canadian content for pipeline projects prior to the Northern Pipeline Act was encouraged by the National Energy Board and has been an important determining factor where competing applications are involved. Other energy project proponents are encouraged to maximize Canadian content, and most publicly say this is their intent. No targets are set by regulatory agencies, nor is performance monitored or enforced except by moral suasion or arguments concerning the rules of good corporate citizenship.

Energy projects are clearly an area where industrial benefit is a national concern. Yet no clear definition of "Canadian" is available. As discussed in the previous chapter, some use the term in reference to any Canadian supplier, even when it only acts as a middleman; others generally are referring to the last point of manufacture in Canada after the cost of imports has been netted out. Given the relaxed way in which the term "Canadian content" is used, it would be most useful to come to an acceptable definition. Depending on the information required, two definitions could be employed. A classification of "Made in" or "Product of" Canada would be useful in identifying most manufactured products, whether jewelry, valves or textiles, as being uniquely Canadian. A "Made in Canada" label would be especially useful to many manufacturers of consumer products under an expanded "Buy Canadian" government program. The intent for these products is to indicate where manufacturing has taken place. Quite a different intent is implied under government or export-oriented procurement. Competing bids are analysed to determine not only the source of manufacture but also the source of components, with Canadian value-added as the principal criteria. The information requirements for each are obviously quite different. As a label for general manufacturing, perhaps no more than the defined level of what constitutes a "substantial" level of manufacturing is required. For government or export procurement programs, especially where competing bids or projects are involved, more detailed analysis is probably needed. This suggests a two-tier approach dependent on the use to which both the definition and the information is to be used:

- *First tier:* to ensure a substantial level of manufacturing.
- *Second tier:* a more detailed analysis of the first as required to identify the content of components.

This distinction can also be useful for energy projects as a means to distinguish those components and bids of relatively low value in relation to total project costs from those of higher value. Any large project inevitably has a few easily identified important procurement decisions and many more relatively insignificant decisions. The first tier is suggested for those of little significance and the second tier for the high-value items. For the smaller procurement purchases, there is, in the words of a senior industrial development officer in Alberta, little sense in "spending a dollar for a nickel's worth of information."

The underlying principal of the exercise is to collect detailed information only when it can be demonstrated as useful to do so. Most observers agree that it is in the high-technology, low-production run equipment that Canadian manufacturers show up most poorly. Detailed information on value-added and foreign content will be useful in documenting exactly *how poorly* and also in identifying clusters of common imports. Such information is not generally available at the moment, and obtaining it is the first step in a program to back out commonly imported components.

It should be noted that several provinces, Alberta in particular, feel no compulsion to settle for a definition any more exacting than one demonstrating that a product is manufactured within their own provincial boundaries.

The manufacturing base in these regions is for the most part relatively undeveloped: attracting any firm, regardless of where components come from, is seen as a very positive and beneficial activity. This is in contrast to Ontario and Quebec's more mature manufacturing community that seeks to expand value-added of existing products by replacing component imports. Needless to say, there is little love lost in the West for Eastern manufacturers. Indeed, the dominant and frankly admitted industrial development attitude in Alberta has provincial officers trying to *back out* imports from Ontario.

Regional industrial development is, of course, a laudable goal; however, the East, and Ontario in particular, must be quick to demonstrate its desire and ability to act on information concerning Western projects in a way that strengthens the industrial base in the East but not at the expense of the industrial aspirations of the West. This will generally take the form of improving Canadian content in products that on economic grounds will continue to be manufactured in the East.

There are two general approaches that can be used: to continue with indirect pressure and moral suasion, or to develop direct subsidy programs for Canadian content.

The first is a continuation of present practice, which holds that the sole function of government is to continue dialogues with energy proponents, identifying manufacturing gaps and generally pointing manufacturers in the right direction. In practice, Canadian content guidelines would be applied outside the general competitive factors of price, quality and delivery. All things being equal, Canadian firms would receive the contract. This approach certainly increases Canadian content (measured by the number of firms) in the bidding lists but not necessarily in awarded contracts.

The second approach attempts to quantify Canadian content as an addition to the conventional competitive bidding practice by penalizing foreign content by a set proportion. Precedents are available with Ontario Hydro, the Federal Department of Supply and Services, and to a lesser extent with Hydro Quebec and British Columbia Hydro. The issue becomes, who pays the premium: proponents or governments? Energy proponents could be expected to be somewhat reluctant to pick up added costs, although if requirements were refined to major components and the criteria developed earlier on what constitutes "Canadian" were applied, total costs of penalizing imports may not be exorbitant:

- In 1978, the "Buy Canadian" policy of Ontario Hydro (see Appendix) resulted in premiums of $561,000 buying contracts to Canadian suppliers worth over $23 million. Premiums in relation to total value of contract awards represented less than three-tenths of 1 per cent. On a project basis, representatives of Foothills Pipe Lines have indicated that research on other domestic projects that have allowed a price premium for Canadian content showed only a 1 to 2 per cent increase in total project costs. Such cost increases would be well within the general 15 per cent contingency allowance on most projects.

- Foothills has developed a procurement policy whereby bids are assessed on a subjective basis, with Canadian content fully specified for all aspects (see Appendix). Evaluation criteria are weighted towards high Canadian content and encourage industrial activity extending into a manufacturer's own component sourcing program. Foothills has indicated a willingness to pay a premium

63

where there is a clear benefit for doing so, such as security of future supply or lower contract administration costs.

At the very least the Foothills model should be encouraged for major projects, but if the industry is incapable of making favourable judgements without excessive cost, governments should consider the application of penalties against foreign content, as in the Ontario Hydro example, and be prepared to pay premiums to the proponent.

This argument attempts to link the cost of assistance to government as the principal beneficiary. By encouraging industrial activity and job creation, major economic benefits accrue to the political host. The level of impact is somewhat uncertain and requires detailed study to maximize benefits to costs and to set the appropriate premium. Rules of thumb used by the Export Development Corporation, however, indicate that every million-dollar increase in Canadian content for manufacturing results in forty-six man-years of employment and that a similar increase in Canadian content for services yields thirty-three man-years.

Premium assistance would be most valuable for those industries and firms marginally non-competitive in price. Firms quoting prices substantially higher than foreign competition, who have a decidedly inferior product or who cannot meet required delivery dates, obviously should not be awarded a contract by any project. Some government support to encourage a better product may be justified under other industrial programs (for research and development, for example) but not generally under a procurement policy. Consideration should also be given to applying the premium in such a way that the evaluation process is used to neutralize any advantage accruing to foreign suppliers who can be identified as receiving support from home governments in terms of subsidization, abnormally low interest rates, or tied concessional financing.

Just as the development of an energy policy and investment timetables is the key pivotal action to be taken by government, the development of explicit procurement policies and a firm resolve to use Canadian firms is the key for the energy industry. Without exception, each energy sector has publicly stated their intent to involve Canadian firms to the maximum extent possible. It should be recognized, however, that such statements alone are motherhood in content; it is difficult to imagine a serious post-Syncrude project proposal that would dare issue a contrary statement.

Maximizing Canadian content requires a carefully thought out procurement policy. One-liners are not enough to demonstrate the corporate resolve. Many observers of the oil and gas industry, in particular, are critical of the actual performance of many project proponents, following their public declaration of general intent. Officials at the Machinery Branch at the Department of Industry, Trade and Commerce have observed the propensity of oil companies to stay with traditional suppliers and contractors, giving only nominal attention to either finding Canadian firms or encouraging them to participate. To date, neither federal nor provincial governments have applied any greater leverage than patriotic appeals and moral suasion to encourage oil companies to patronize Canadian suppliers. To be fair, there is noticeable improvement in the performance of most proponents, particularly in the tar sands and oil refining, but maximum participation of Canadians regardless of energy sector will require more than general intent; *how* the intent is to be made real must be specified. Too often large projects derive their procurement policy from the policy of the lead company without recognizing the often substantial differences in material availability and sourcing problems encountered by particular projects against the overall corporate activity.

As already mentioned, models of procurement policy are not unknown to the energy industry; Ontario Hydro and Foothills Pipe Lines can be held up as serious attempts to make purchasing policy explicit. Although quite different in approach, both set the ground rules for maximizing Canadian content.

Not surprisingly, many of the best Canadian content performances in the energy sector have been achieved by those groups that have a history of Canadian content guidelines. Ontario Hydro, for example, averages 85 – 90 per cent (excluding turbine generator sets), and the pipeline community also is in the 80 – 90 per cent Canadian content range. A very fortunate side effect of setting guidelines is that procurement officers are constantly searching for new Canadian sources as an essential and rewarding part of their job and not as a vaguely defined, cumbersome task.

In fact, the attitudes of those in charge of procurement are probably as important as the rules established. Where product deficiencies are present, either in availability, quality or delivery, procurement officers are the first to know and are often in a position to help develop future supply from currently uncompetitive firms. In the opinion of a senior representative of the Purchasing Department at TransCanada PipeLines (TCPL), the purchaser's job is not simply to buy equipment and materials but also to develop Canadian sources. The success of this approach is demonstrated by the increase of Canadian content for TCPL projects from under 25 per cent in 1956 to over 90 per cent today, with secure supplies at required specifications for present and future requirements. Of course, TCPL's capability has evolved over time, but by developing a shopping list of major needs and through direct contact with potential suppliers, the improvement has been dramatic. According to this official, manufacturers can be coaxed along by demonstrating how forecasts of equipment needs have been developed and by emphasizing the companys' commitment to buy in Canada.

Just as important as one-on-one dialogue is the judicious use of business trade conferences. Representatives of the Foothills and Alsands projects have indicated the success of these conferences in providing the manufacturing community with project shopping lists and preliminary specifications. The result of the dialogue has been a greater understanding of problems and opportunities by both parties and higher estimates of Canadian content for each project. Most projects, of course, do not approach the size and complexity of an Alsands or Foothills. Nonetheless, all energy sectors' equipment requirements continuously evolve as do the capabilities of the manufacturing community. Periodic seminars, perhaps hosted by associations, will help keep buyer/seller information current.

"Buy Canadian" procurement programs should be developed by manufacturers as well as by government and energy proponents. The ethic should be encouraged at all levels, possibly through joint industry/government campaigns to encourage manufacturers to look for Canadian suppliers for currently imported components. There is a need to determine the basic factors that cause manufacturers to favour imports over domestic production and to reverse their operation where possible. Direct approaches and manufacturers' conferences will be required. Government and project proponents could also add the "Buy Canadian" record of suppliers to the purchasing criteria used in awarding contracts.

Minimizing Imports

The manufacturing community has performed well in supplying the energy sectors with equipment and machinery, but there is always room for improvement. Additional improvement may be achieved by ensuring that a few persistent impediments are removed. Specifically, technological control over major resource exploitation projects has in the past been dominated by foreign firms. A second area of concern has been the extent to which foreign manufacturers use support from home governments to underbid domestic firms. Another way of minimizing imports is to encourage project proponents to recognize some basic limitations of Canadian manufacturers and to plan accordingly. Finally, the federal government should implement a comprehensive import substitution program.

A basic issue in all energy sectors is the extent to which Canadians are capable of managing the design and construction of major projects over the next decade. Maximizing Canadian content of engineering, procurement and construction (EPC) functions is the first step toward higher overall Canadian content. Canadian construction and design firms have proven experience and an international reputation in such fields as mining, hydroelectric and nuclear development, pipelines, forestry, transportation and communication. In 1977 these sectors alone represented $570 million in billings to consulting engineers, $127 million of which came from international work. Energy-related billings represented 22 per cent of total fees collected in that year. Of these billings 15 per cent came from international projects (see Table 3-1). The competence of the construction and engineering community is attested to by continuing international success in these areas.

TABLE 3-1
BILLINGS OF CANADIAN CONSULTING ENGINEERS, 1977

	$ Millions	% of Total	Export (% of Sector)
Energy related	263	22	15
Buildings	204	17	4
Municipal	186	16	5
Mining	109	9	30
Plant process	97	8	35
Transportation	96	8	16
Forestry	88	7	38
Air and seaports	30	3	27
Telecommunications	14	1	43
Miscellaneous	103	9	11
Total	1,190	100	17

Source: Developed from Peter Barnard Associates, *Consulting Engineering in Canada, Overview and Prospects,* Department of Industry, Trade & Commerce, 1978.

Industry observers, however, have become increasingly concerned about the lack of opportunity so far for Canadian-controlled firms to compete for lead roles in several types of major energy projects in the oil and gas industry: most notably in oil sands projects, refineries and gas processing plants. Large, multinational firms have overwhelmingly been given prime contracting roles for these projects.

There are reasons for this, of course: the principal factor is simply the way energy-related construction and engineering firms in Canada have related to their traditional clients. Utilities and pipelines, in particular, have a development history that has emphasized the division of responsibility among all participants:

- Engineering and construction are contracted separately to specialized firms; project proponents generally have in-house capability as well.
- The critical functions of procurement and overall project management are exercised by the project proponent.

The result has been for Canadian firms to become specialists within their own sphere. Very few engineering firms, for example, have construction specialists and only a few construction firms have a significant engineering department. In addition, only limited large-project managment skills have been developed.

The preference of the major firms in the oil and gas industry shows a sharp contrast. Although large, their approach is to buy process-related experience rather than building projects themselves. They feel it is far cheaper and more expedient to contract with one firm that will be responsible for all aspects of the work: in-house and contracted engineering; procurement of all equipment and supplies; construction contracts; and, most important, work scheduling and project management. To paraphrase one industry observer, the multinational oil companies pick a project, decide where they want it, shepherd the project through the regulatory process, pick the best bid and have it built. It takes nerve, confidence and considerable financial resources to sign a performance contract for several billion dollars of work—as is the case for the oil sands mega-projects. The stakes involved in these projects are high and understandably project proponents prefer to contract with well-established companies with experience in managing large projects. Nonetheless, it is essential to develop effective Canadian participation in these projects. Increasing Canadian content will have important benefits:

- greater domestic control over the development of large resource projects by having Canadian firms in charge;
- greater and more responsible employment of Canadian engineers and contractors;
- development of increased expertise by Canadian firms, thereby broadening their potential export markets and generally increasing their international competitiveness;
- Canadian firms and engineers would have a better appreciation of

domestic equipment availability and manufacturing capabilities, aiding the procurement process.

The federal government, along with some provincial governments, has recognized the shortcomings of Canadian firms and is constantly encouraging project proponents to increase Canadian content. Moral suasion has generally been successful in incrementally adding to the work-load of Canadian firms. The lead role, however, remains with large multinational and fully integrated engineering-construction firms.

But the fact is that Canadian firms at present are not matching the requirements the market demands in executing these large projects. Two strategic options are available:

- to alter the market requirements, forcing a break in the traditional use of one contracting firm;
- or, to encourage Canadian firms to grow to match the management capabilities of the competition.

In fact, the industry's tendency is a combination of both with greatest emphasis on developing management expertise. The project receiving the greatest criticism for the use of a foreign EPC firm was Syncrude. Although estimates vary, it would appear that roughly two-thirds of all engineering work and virtually all construction was subcontracted to Canadian firms. At issue is that while thousands of Canadians did most of the work, Bechtel (the prime contractor) received the credit and the international reputation. Any questions concerning the ability or talent of Canadian firms to do the design engineering work for this and any other project have long since been put to rest. In fact, a senior official of the Consulting Engineering Association of Alberta believes the membership have never been so busy and are constantly improving their skills. This official also believes, and it is a widely held viewpoint, that there is still no Canadian firm capable of taking on projects as large as Alsands or Cold Lake. The pieces are all there but no firm has under one roof sufficient staff or financial resources to take on projects much larger than $500 million.

Increasingly over the past several years, these shortcomings are being addressed through joint ventures as an attempt to break the historical pattern. Although joint ventures are not a preferable option from the perspective of the oil and gas industry, some accommodation in response to government pressure is evident. Two alternative philosophies in forming these joint ventures can be recognized:

- Permanent joint ventures. Half-a-dozen large Canadian firms have entered into partnership with international firms. International stature and broad experience tend to be maximized. To date, this strategy has been unsuccessful.

- Project joint ventures. Several Canadian and foreign firms join forces for a project with varying degrees of project responsibility and one principal contractor. These are gaining credibility and acceptance and are the arrangements currently in place for the Alsands and Cold Lake projects.

Even for the latter, some variation is evident between the arrangements for Alsands and Cold Lake consortiums, as Table 3-2 suggests. It is debatable which approach will turn out to be the most successful. Both will give many Canadian companies an established track record and valuable experience. The stated government objective, in both Alberta and at the federal level, is to have the next mega-project headed by a Canadian firm. Given the evolutionary nature of past industry performance and the more recent contracting assignments noted above, any one of several firms may be in this position. According to several observers the firm that wins this role will be the one that can demonstrate the management skills necessary to bring the project in "on time and on budget."

TABLE 3-2
TWO CONSORTIUM ARRANGEMENTS FOR LARGE PROJECTS

Alsands	*Cold Lake*
Three Participating Contractors	Prime Contractor and Four Participating Contractors
• two being 100% Canadian • all having specified tasks • Alsands as parent company taking stronger role in overall management • emphasis on project management and subcontracted design work	• prime contractor responsible for overall project management • each of four participating contractors are Canadian, responsible for as yet unspecified tasks. They will provide all management and design/construction

The project management theme should be increasingly stressed across all energy sectors, for similar Canadian shortcomings are evident in refinery projects, the petrochemical industry, and may occur in offshore oil and gas development—when and if the exploratory phase of development evolves into field production. Firms are judged by their overall performance record—not solely on performance in one isolated sector. Cost-conscious clients, whether domestic or foreign, are apt to be wary of contractors with no management experience, even if their credentials are otherwise impeccable. If Canadian firms wish to compete successfully in new fields as prime contractors rather than as subcontractors overseas, and if they intend to take an active role in solving the technical problems of domestic energy projects over the next twenty years, whether it be in oil sands, offshore production facilities or developing tidal power, these management skills must be developed.

More of this project management experience could be gained if utilities, other government agencies and the pipeline community de-emphasized their traditional project management role and encouraged greater participation by contractors. Each of these groups has considerable in-house experience, much of which could be usefully made available to private firms under a program of seconding key individuals to the management team.

Ensuring Fair Domestic Competition

The energy industry requires very sophisticated equipment, and many manufacturers have responded by developing uniquely Canadian products. The success of such developments is generally preconditioned by a strong domestic market. The unfortunate fact is, however, that trade practices of other countries do at times impede the development of *our own* domestic industrial base. There is evidence of this, for instance, in the utility market for industrial electrical equipment.

The electrical industry has two distinct industrial markets: those supplying equipment to the utilities (turbines, generators, transformers and transmission equipment) and those supplying other industries (motors and industrial control equipment). According to a senior staff economist with the Electrical and Electronics Manufacturers Association of Canada (EEMAC), the utility market up to the past several years has traditionally been stronger than that for industrial equipment. More recently, however, the utility market has weakened as a result of both a general downturn in utilities expenditure programs across the country and significant and successful foreign competition.

The domestic utility market is made up of twenty-one electric power utilities plus a few companies that generate power for their own use. Although seemingly a large domestic base from which to operate, in fact only four make up 80 per cent of the market (see Table 3-3). At first glance, the impression is of a highly concentrated market. Looking deeper, however, we find it highly fragmented, essentially as a result of the procurement practices of the provincial utilities, which account for roughly 90 per cent of all utility purchases of electrical equipment.

TABLE 3-3
INSTALLED ELECTRICAL CAPACITY IN CANADA, 1978

	MW Installed	% Domestic Capacity
Ontario Hydro	25,667	35
Hydro Quebec	16,564	23
Newfoundland	6,932	10
B.C. Hydro	9,112	13
Total	58,275	81
Total Canada	72,873	100

Source: National Energy Board, *Canadian Electrical Utilities, Analysis of Generation and Trends,* 1978.

Utilities are first and foremost in the business of producing electricity at the lowest cost possible to their customers, and they must naturally consider their own self-interest in making purchasing decisions. For most, buying at the lowest cost is reinforced by provincial legislation. As seen in Appendix Table 1, only three utilities, Ontario Hydro, Hydro Quebec and British Columbia Hydro, offer any price premium for Canadian manufacturers, and all offer the largest advantage to firms located within their own boundaries, with other national firms receiving a lower level of support. The others operate on the lowest-evaluated bid concept. Of course, other things being equal, they will all select bids from firms within their own boundaries.

The result, according to EEMAC is twofold: first, those provinces offering relatively protected markets encourage the fragmentation of the domestic manufacturing market. Terms and conditions compatible with the capabilities of local suppliers are generally applied. Secondly, provinces with a less-developed electrical products industry leave the door open to foreign firms capable of providing terms and conditions that cannot be matched by domestic firms. The effects of the former condition have already been discussed, but the latter is also cause for some concern.

Our domestic utility market policies are clearly at odds with the utility practices of other developed countries. Japan and the major trading countries in Europe require that purchasing policies of their utilities be consistent with national mandates to promote industrial benefit, with strong support given to national equipment manufacturers. A senior electrical advisor with the Federal Department of Energy, Mines and Resources suggests that Canadian firms cannot enter these markets at any price and that protected markets allow foreign manufacturers to cover fixed costs and offer low export prices based on marginal pricing. In addition, many governments will support their manufacturers by direct project financing at subsidized interest rates, or with price guarantees that allow firms to offer firm prices even during periods of high inflation. As indicated by representatives of Ontario Hydro (see previous chapter), there is general world over-capacity in heavy electrical goods and manufacture, and foreign activity of this kind is increasing. Based on these comments, the free market approach adopted by Canadian utilities would seem to run counter to international competitive realities.

While there is little firm and well-documented evidence on the extent to which Canadian manufacturers are losing business as a result of subsidized foreign bids on domestic contracts, it is known that over the past several years British Columbia, Manitoba and New Brunswick have made large purchases of thermal and hydro turbines, runners and generators from Japan and the U.S.S.R. Many in the industry feel that other countries have developed and refined their technology and gained export experience in Canadian markets, even when Canadian firms would have been able to compete successfully were it not for foreign "dumping." This opinion, although somewhat subjective, is often repeated and deserves government attention.

It is clear, however, that Canada *is* a net importer of much of the equipment used by the utilities. In 1976 imports exceeded exports by a ratio of 4 to 1, with imports representing 33 per cent of the domestic market, considerably higher than the 24 per cent experienced a decade earlier; these imports contributed to a $312 million trade deficit. (See Table 3-4.) The Electrical Industry Task Force report from which these statistics are drawn concludes "that the cause of the deficit is not so much a low rate of exports, but rather a very high penetration of our domestic markets by foreign manufacturers. . . . Canada is the only country among the large producers with a negative trade balance in electrical products." Thus, the "open door" procurement policy of many Canadian utilities is contributing to a growing deficit in industrial electrical equipment and is inhibiting Canadian manufacturers from developing a stronger domestic base.

TABLE 3-4
INDUSTRIAL ELECTRICAL EQUIPMENT MARKETS
(in millions of 1976 $'s)

	Domestic Market	Shipments	Exports	Imports	Trade Balance
1965	464	376	25	113	− 88
1976	1,252	940	104	416	− 312
Change	147%	150%	316%	268%	254%

Source: Electrical Industry Task Force, *Report on the Canadian Electrical Products Industry*, 1978.

The extent to which similar practices are widespread in other energy industries is unknown, but given the high-technology character of many products, they are likely to be quite frequent. It is an important problem. Canada should use its vast market opportunities to develop its own firms. Certainly, action taken to neutralize or prevent the adverse impact of foreign subsidies, concessional financing packages and marginal pricing will reduce uncertainty and encourage domestic investment as well as replace imports and strengthen industry's potential for export.

Planning around Canadian Limitations
Limited domestic markets and the generally small size of Canadian firms compared to international competitors necessitate some careful planning by proponents if Canadians are to participate in a meaningful way. Several lessons have already been learned and should be applied to future projects wherever possible.

Equipment requirements should not be viewed in isolation but in conjunction with other projects. Although there is general agreement that most requirements can be met if investments are staged and enough lead time is available, it is not at all clear what will happen if projects become bunched together. Most likely the physical resources of many Canadian manufacturers would not be sufficient, and equipment and materials otherwise easily sourced in Canada would have to be purchased from foreign suppliers.

Wherever possible, components should be standardized. Wherever clusters of equipment requirements (valves, pumps and fittings, for example) are identified, they should be reviewed by project proponents and manufacturers alike to assess the need for design specifications that may show only minor variation. Small adjustments in project design may in the end yield larger production runs, lower prices and more readily available domestic sources of supply.

The size of bid packages should be within reach of Canadian firms. Whether one bid of $10 million is tendered or two of $5 million each can make a big difference in the number of Canadian firms who can submit bids. Bid sizes should be optimized to reflect a compromise between both the size limitations of Canadian firms and the increased administrative cost of handling submissions from more firms. Both the Alsands and Cold Lake projects have indicated their intention to keep the size of bids smaller than was the case with Syncrude and also to break some requirements down to the component level. A broader base of supply will result.

Preassembly and modularization also encourages the smaller bidder. Edmonton, the staging area for the Alsands project, for example, will have 2,400 employees involved in preassembly activities. More small suppliers can be involved, and transportation for large equipment is easier. Thus, Alsands believes preassembly saves money.

Canadian firms should be considered when sourcing replacement parts. Canadian firms may not be capable of supplying some equipment requirements but may very easily develop a supply capability for replacement components during the lifetime of the machinery. A number of projects using essentially the same equipment (draglines for coal mining and oil sands development, for example) could open new markets.

Most of the above recommendations are aimed at ensuring that products already available in Canada are given the opportunity to be bought. A second and just as rewarding opportunity is to develop new products to take the place of imports.

The predominant characteristic of much of the equipment required for the energy industry, especially for machinery, is that their markets are international. Indigenous machinery capability is an important part of mature economies and most industrialized countries have strong machinery-producing capabilities competing for a broad range of requirements. Table 3-5 shows that Canada is one of the highest net importers of all the major machinery-producing countries.

The Canadian market is typical of developed countries in that it encompasses a broad and very diverse range of machinery needs. The energy industry market reflects this diversity. The high import level observed for Canada arises in part because of the huge variety of requirements and the fact that quantitative demands for each type and size of machinery are much lower than is the case for other major producing countries. All of this points to two things:

- First, that an import substitution program must be developed to allow Canadians the opportunity to more completely meet our own requirements.

75

TABLE 3-5
MACHINERY TRADE BY MAJOR
PRODUCING COUNTRIES

Country	% of Domestic Requirements Imported	% of Production Exported
U.S.	10	17
Japan	10	24
West Germany	34	63
Britain	34	50
France	50	45
Sweden	50	59
Canada	60	30

Source: Department of Industry, Trade and Commerce, *A Report by the Sector Task Force on the Canadian Machinery Industry*, 1978.

- Second, that there are large international markets for successful Canadian firms who can use their domestic base and experience.

Substituting imports and pursuing exports are both aimed at the same goal: to improve the manufacturing market. A strong export orientation needs a viable domestic base, and the domestic base is filled out by the economies of scale reached by entering export markets.

Complete self-sufficiency through an import substitution program in machinery products is obviously an unrealistic goal. As shown in the above table, it has not been achieved by any industrialized country. However, the table does indicate Canada is lagging behind other countries—other countries with high imports are also high exporters.

Although it is statistically difficult to separate the requirements of the energy industry from the total market, Table 3-6 gives an indication of the significance of the level of imports for machinery and equipment commonly used by the energy industry. The following list reflects various types of export opportunity the Canadian market offers foreign suppliers:

- Items for which Canadian firms are competing but not always successfully. For example, indigenous hydroelectric and industrial gas turbines have been developed in Canada and are being successfully marketed overseas. Import penetration is said to result from various types of foreign government financial assistance to exporters.

TABLE 3-6
CANADIAN IMPORTS BY COMMODITY
(in thousands of $'s)

Equipment	Application	1970	1979*	Annual Growth(%)
Hydraulic turbines & parts	Hydro generation	2,476	30,213	33
Gas turbines	Industrial & pipe-lines	10,222	26,232	11
Well-drilling machinery	Oil & gas explora-tion	39,054	300,606	25
Petroleum & gas field production equipment	Oil & gas produc-tion	11,450	96,367	27
Valves	Industrial & most energy sectors	44,085	101,650	10
Fittings	Industrial & most energy sectors	33,495	120,356	15
Zirconium alloys	Nuclear fuel supply systems	3,667	13,201	15
Diesel, semi-diesel engines & parts	Stationary power & construction equip-ment	25,471	133,186	20
Construction equip-ment	All construction activities	166,947	721,710	18

*As of the end of November.

Source: Statistics Canada, *Imports by Commodities*, various issues.

77

- Items characterized by widely divergent specifications, varying from project to project. Valves and fittings, in particular, are required with tremendous variation of sizes, quality and alloy contents. The larger and technically more sophisticated requirements are imported.
- Equipment requirements for which Canadian firms have not been able to match order levels. Record levels of investment in exploration and production in the oil and gas industry have required equipment to be imported. Newly created fabrication facilities in Alberta will offset future imports as manufacturers see greater and continuing opportunities to supply Canadian land-based drill rigs. A large proportion of the $300 million worth of imported exploration equipment results from offshore drill rigs and many ships, which continue to be largely imported.
- Requirements which are not available in Canada. The area of construction equipment and large diesel engines, in particular, has very few Canadian firms actively pursuing markets. Virtually all construction equipment for the pipeline industry and for hydroelectric projects is foreign based, for example.

Even this partial list of common imports suggests the volume represented by import requirements. The total imports of machinery products in 1978 were in fact over $5.6 billion, with an annual trade deficit of $3.5 million or 23 per cent of the total domestic deficit on end products. Using the rule of thumb of forty-six man-years for every million dollars of Canadian content, if only a quarter of the deficit were replaced by Canadian activity, about 40,000 new jobs would be created.

Developing new products to replace current or future imports will require that several preconditions to domestic manufacture be in place:

- Additional tariff support for equipment items included under oil and gas exploration and refining and construction equipment is required. Firms supplying oil- and gas-related equipment, for example, require a 10 per cent share of the domestic market before tariffs are established as a "Made in Canada" product. But 90 per cent of machinery firms in Canada have fewer than a hundred employees and account for only 35 per cent of total shipments. Most are capable of competing in the domestic market. But when a Canadian product approaches the 10 per cent market share, incremental pricing by foreign firms (mainly U.S.) begins to be observed. The large U.S. firms currently active in export all started as small service and manufacturing shops that grew as their domestic market expanded. An open-door tariff policy in our oil and gas industry may impede local machine shops from growing in the same manner. Action to remove inequities in the tariff structure should provide assistance to industry, increase the range of products manufactured in Canada and help obtain a larger share of the domestic market for items already produced here.

- Canadian firms require more indigenous technology. Without a competent technology base, Canada has no chance to extend its technological control over the new energy sectors or to extend an advantage internationally. The tar sands and offshore oil and gas development are two areas in particular that require research and the advancement of uniquely Canadian extraction and development technologies. The parent-subsidiary relationships of many firms involved in the machinery industry point to particular problems in extending the technological sovereignty of Canadian firms, particularly where competing products become involved. Nonetheless, new or improved technology will be required to fully develop our energy resources. Canadian subsidiaries should approach parent companies for regional or global marketing rights to selected new products or designs. Strong Canadian government resolve and support in offsetting research and development costs must be available to support the argument.

  In addition, the production of some equipment currently not manufactured in Canada will involve a costly learning period. To some extent procurement policies that levy percentage penalties against imports will alleviate higher initial costs of production. Consideration should also be given to providing investment assistance while new producers endeavour to reduce production costs to levels required to meet import competition.

- Where developing a new product is not justified, using foreign technology for products to be produced in Canada is a minimum strategy. Rather than simply importing equipment at the project level, Canadian firms unable to justify long-term research and development programs should carefully monitor international technology advances and be prepared to enter into licensing arrangements. Although admittedly a short-term strategy, license agreements at least open the possibility for some component sourcing in Canada and can lead to incentives for other firms to innovate and create a totally Canadian product.

A similar case can be made for encouraging the fabrication of components within Canada. Again it is a minimal and short-term approach but it does create jobs and does allow the opportunity to

79

replace imports by Canadian components. The fabrication of drilling rigs is a case in point. Where, previously, entire rigs were imported, new fabrication facilities are now permitting upward of 80 per cent Canadian content with only the more sophisticated equipment still being imported.

Promoting Exports

It is obvious that improvements in industrial competitiveness that result from import substitution will also lead to an expanded capability to compete in export markets. This is important because domestic markets alone are not likely to support large-scale investment in new facilities. There is good reason to pursue the dual objective of simultaneously penetrating both domestic and export markets.

Industrial opportunities related to energy investment are obviously not confined to Canada but exist in virtually every country in the world. This implies both huge potential markets and established competition. The Canadian advantage is the diversity of domestic energy sources that we may become masters of: ranging from land-based and offshore oil and gas to oil sands, from heavy oils through nuclear, tidal and hydro-generated electricity to transmitting electricity, oil and gas over vast distances. There is opportunity in the renewable energy field as well: including solar, wind and biomass sources. Though Canada is not alone in exploiting any of these, few other countries may boast of the opportunity to develop such a broad range of energy sources.

As stated in the previous chapter, such a huge diversity of project types also implies a huge diversity of equipment and machinery requirements. Those requirements in turn imply a wide range of technologies and types of manufacturing facilities. These include high investment, specialized machinery with high levels of design and custom manufacturing for turbines, generators, transformers, specialist valves and fittings, et cetera. These production systems are applied to very specific equipment requirements for specific project types and the product is unique from order to order.

At the other end of the spectrum, there are mass production techniques for conventional valves, fittings, wire and cable, capacitors, et cetera. These production systems and products have a somewhat more standard application for energy projects and often for other industrial applications.

Whichever the category, internationally successful Canadian exporters of energy-related equipment have one thing in common: they have developed a unique technology. The success stories are few in number, but Canadian industry is internationally recognized in such areas as hydro generators, transformers, circuit breakers, long-distance transmission systems, industrial gas turbines and nuclear valves and pumps. In many of these cases (hydro generators and gas turbines in particular) rationalization agreements between Canadian subsidiaries and the parent company have allowed the Canadian firms full and generally indigenous research and development programs along with world marketing rights. In all these examples, however, companies have developed unique equipment and capabilities and have marketed them successfully in Canada and abroad.

Indigenous technology, although the key requirement, is also the key problem within the Canadian context. A recent report by the Export Promotion Review Committee (the Hatch Report), points out the traditional lack of an indigenous technology base within Canada.

> Canada's dependence on outsiders for technology is of long duration. It is evidenced by a persistent net outflow of technology royalties. Most royalty flows are between parent and subsidiary, but a number of Canadian-owned firms have also found it much more attractive to compete at home against multinational subsidiaries by licensing technology from abroad rather than doing their own design and product development work. A small market, protected from the full blast of international competition, tends to elicit this kind of corporate strategy from indigenous firms. One resulting problem is that most products manufactured in Canada are designed elsewhere, and component sourcing follows the locus of design. What then has Canada to export? If most of what is made here is a more expensive copy of what is made in the U.S. how can Canadian firms possibly compete in export markets?[1]

The two most important manufacturing groups supplying the energy sector are dominated by subsidiaries representing multinational or large U.S. corporations: 50 per cent and 70 per cent of total output in the machinery and electrical equipment sectors respectively are produced by foreign-owned companies. Whether or not foreign ownership is healthy for the Canadian economy is beyond the scope of this report, but subsidiaries *are* somewhat disadvantaged in developing an exportable product. Most, if not all, of these subsidiaries were originally conceived in response to high preferential Canadian tariffs designed to promote Canadian production for domestic consumption.[2] Production technologies, as the Hatch Report suggests, have generally been patterned after the parent company's on a scale suitable to smaller Canadian markets. As a result of the recently concluded Tokyo round of GATT negotiations, however, there has been a general relaxation of tariffs. The consequences of such reductions to subsidiary operations is not known exactly, but for subsidiaries producing virtually the same product with the same technology as the parent, a less competitive operation may result. Gaining access to indigenous technology and product lines, along the pattern of the successful examples noted earlier, will give subsidiaries an advantage in the domestic market. And negotiating marketing rights to that technology will enable a greater contribution to Canada's export effort. The Hatch Report, on the question of ownership and its effects on Canadian production, suggests that policies should emphasize positive incentives for Canadian firms so that they might become internationally competitive, rather than promote negative measures to constrain the multinationals. Developing technological sovereignty is clearly the key requirement.

Government Resolve Is Essential
To be successful, Canadian exporters need the support for their initiatives and a commitment of assistance from the government. If industry is to become more clearly the master of its own technology, it must be recognized that the high-technology machinery and electrical industries are competing in international markets, against established and often much larger international firms.

Concessional financing by foreign governments should continue to be actively discouraged. Given current world overcapacity in various sectors of the machinery and industrial electrical product markets, the established pattern of concessional export financing by foreign governments can be expected to continue and perhaps become even more noticeable. If the free trade philosophy of current government policy is to survive, it must be recognized that such financing offers advantages to foreign suppliers that Canadian firms generally cannot match. The government must at least monitor the level of financing coming into Canada, with the aim of neutralizing its effects where direct competition with Canadian products can be demonstrated.

Should attempts to reduce these financing arrangements be unsuccessful, alterations to the conventional export approach adopted by Canada should be considered so that Canada can more completely match the assistance provided by other countries. As shown in Table 3-7, Canadian export assistance is substantially lower than that of most other trading nations. Canadian government support is notably lacking in the following areas:

- insurance against currency fluctuations;
- tax rebates and incentives for exports;
- tax exemption of foreign branch income.

The Hatch report, cited earlier, makes the case that although tax incentive for particular groups generally goes against the grain of government policy, it is required not simply as favoured assistance but

TABLE 3-7
NATIONAL EXPORT ASSISTANCE FOR SELECTED COUNTRIES

	France	Germany	UK	Japan	Italy	USA	Canada
Insurance against currency fluctuations	Yes	Yes	Yes	Yes	Yes	No	No
Tax rebate on exports	Yes	Yes	Yes	No	Yes	No	No
Indirect tax incentives for exports	Yes	Yes	Yes	No	Yes	No	No
Tax exemptions	Yes	Yes	Yes	No	Yes	No	No
Insurance against export losses	Yes	Yes	Yes	Yes	No	No	Yes
Direct export tax incentives	Yes	No	Yes	Yes	No	No	No
Partial or total exemption of foreign branch income	Yes	Yes	No	No	No	No	No
Deferral of export income	Yes	Yes	No	Yes	No	Yes	Partly

Source: H. Peter Guttman, *The International Consultant* (New York: McGraw-Hill, 1976).

in order to put Canadian firms on an equal footing with their key international competitors. The report goes on to name six tax incentives:

- inflated write-off for tax purposes on the full spectrum of innovation activities, not just R and D;
- deferral of export earnings to take account of the length of time receivables are outstanding;
- inflated tax write-off for export marketing expenditures;
- loss carry-back privileges for large contracts involving long-term progress payments;
- exemption of foreign dividends from Canadian tax regardless of the tax treaty status of the host country;
- more liberal tax treatment of Canadians working abroad in the interests of Canadian trade.

Export support services require ongoing coordination. A common criticism of exporters is the difficulty faced in moving through the diversity of federal agencies that have export trade programs. There is little coordination between the five major federal departments or agencies—the Canadian Commercial Corporation (CCC), the Canadian International Development Agency (CIDA), the Export Development Agency (EDA), Industry, Trade and Commerce and External Affairs—nor even within their component branches. The Hatch Report recommends the formation of the "Export Trade Development Board," which would consist of both private and public sector members whose function would be to focus and coordinate export efforts, and develop and monitor export performance based on agreed policies.

Export marketing support should be a key function of foreign postings. Several observers of export programs are frankly critical of the second-class treatment given to trade promotion, compared to the more traditional diplomatic functions. This is in contrast to the apparently more aggressive marketing approach taken by other countries. Many of the association executives and government employees contacted for this study are increasingly concerned that Canadian firms are missing many opportunities because of a "lack of hustle" by the Trade Commissioner Service (TCS). Several corrective measures should be considered:

- Trade commissioners and commercial officers must be thoroughly versed in the capabilities of domestic suppliers. A comprehensive sourcing information system and more frequent familiarization tours are required.
- A mechanism allowing more complete monitoring of projects in

84

host countries and the sharing of such information with Canadian manufacturers should be established.

- A greater continuity of support could be ensured by reducing the frequency of posting rotations of trade commissioners.
- Trade in general should be recognized as having a very important role in foreign posts.

Canadian firms must become more competitive in bidding on major capital projects abroad. The leading edge toward creating opportunities for these projects is provided by the engineering and construction firms in a position to offer full engineering, design and construction services. Increasingly, the tendency for energy projects around the world is to require "turnkey" capability. The magnitude of these projects, however, poses serious problems for Canadian firms. (Billion-dollar contracts are common, $250 million contracts are considered modest.) Marketing and promotion costs, in relation to the risk, are high, as are the costs of monitoring the overseas market environment. Just preparing the bid may involve several million dollars. These pre-bid expenses are at present covered by the Federal Program for Export and Market Development (PEMD), which will reimburse one-half of the pre-bid costs on approved applications. Further, the costs of winning the bid in a high inflation environment or in uncertain currency markets can lead firms to inflate project costs to offset potential losses caused by factors unrelated to performance. Unlike other countries, Canadian firms have no access to risk-sharing insurance programs sponsored by government. The limited capital structure of most Canadian firms could lead to bankruptcy from even small miscalculations. On the other hand, an excessive contingency allowance can make Canadian bids uncompetitive in relation to foreign firms with access to insurance incentives. Finally, domestic project management skills have generally not developed to the point where a Canadian firm can successfully demonstrate experience with large projects.

If Canada (and hence the manufacturing industries) is to share adequately in the growing turnkey capital project market, Canadian firms will need ready access to information on project proposals, support against unforeseen risks of inflation and currency adjustments, and an expanded role in project management on domestic energy projects.

Conclusions

With a minimum of $210 billion in energy investment and $67 billion in equipment requirements over the next decade, it is difficult to overestimate the significance of this emerging industrial opportunity. At the heart of the opportunity is the extent to which the resolve to maximize Canadian content will be present. Governments must take a lead role and must demonstrate an unfailing commitment to the support of Canadian firms. Just as important will be the actions taken by energy proponents and the Canadian industry itself.

The key function of government will be to ensure that the necessary preconditions for industrial participation are present. An energy policy and investment strategy are essential to provide clear signals to Canadian industry. Production capacity and research and development efforts will have to be expanded to meet the industrial opportunity. Forward planning by Canadian industry demands a decisive sense of direction for the national energy future.

Canadian firms require assurance that they will be given a fair chance in the awarding of equipment and service contracts. The mechanisms for providing this assurance are varied and include: moral suasion, such as that proffered by the federal Advisory Committee on Industrial Benefit from Natural Resources Development; legislation, such as the Northern Pipeline Act and the anticipated Oil and Gas Act; or the development of a national procurement policy penalizing excessive or unwarranted foreign content. The British and Norwegian experience in the North Sea has demonstrated the substantial industrial benefit that may accrue given the resolve to maximize domestic content.

An indigenous technology base must be encouraged to maximize both domestic and export opportunities. The oil sands and frontier and offshore development provide opportunities for Canadians to be in the forefront of technological advances.

Energy proponents must demonstrate a resolve to use Canadian firms wherever practicable. Procurement policies must be developed in a thoughtful and purposeful manner. Procurement from Canadian sources must be viewed as beneficial in its own right, not as an inconvenience to established procurement patterns. Finding and encouraging Canadian suppliers will be the ultimate test of project proponents' resolve to maximize Canadian content. Not surprisingly, the best Canadian content performances come from those energy sectors that view Canadian procurement as an essential part of the purchasing process. Project planning should recognize Canadian limitations and be designed accordingly. Limited domestic markets and the generally small size of domestic firms compared to international competitors must be recognized. Effective planning is required to standardize equipment specifications wherever possible, to ensure that the size of bid packages is within reach of Canadian firms, and to identify Canadian firms capable of supplying replacement parts.

Canadian industry itself must be more aggressive in promoting its products and technical excellence. The "Buy Canadian" procurement ethic must extend into industry. Developing Canadian suppliers of product components is as essential as encouraging energy proponents to seek out Canadian firms for their projects.

Industry must be prepared to face the demand for the specialized and unique technology and equipment required by the energy sector. Capitalizing on the energy opportunities in the Eighties will often necessitate a shift in marketing focus away from the domestic and into international markets in order to achieve economies of scale. Technological excellence will be required for both. Some firms will have to negotiate licensing agreements, subsidiaries will have to negotiate international marketing rights with parent companies, and, hopefully, many other firms will develop research and development programs consistent with the needs of the 1980s. Past performance in the CANDU nuclear industry has demonstrated that Canadian firms can respond to very diverse, exacting and high-technology requirements.

Finally, Canadian firms must aggressively pursue the opportunities provided by the energy sector. Preconditions for their involvement can be established by government and project proponents, but only the firms themselves can convert the opportunities into hard orders. In the end, high Canadian content in energy investment will depend on the aggressiveness with which Canadian firms respond to the challenge.

Appendix

Canadian Content Policies

Federal Government Agencies

Governments are large purchasers of equipment and materials. Provincial governments favour provincial over national suppliers and the federal government favours national over international suppliers. The Federal Department of Supply and Services provides a 10 per cent penalty on the value of imported components. Foreign content is analysed to one supplier down from the point of last manufacture.

Export programs sponsored by government agencies such as the Export Development Corporation (EDC) and the Canadian International Development Agency (CIDA) are also mandated to maximize Canadian content. CIDA, for example, maintains an overall average of 80 per cent for all purchases and a minimum of 67 per cent for overseas projects. Manufacturers are required to supply Canadian content estimates to the last point of manufacture, but few are checked and no penalties are assessed for failing to achieve estimates. Spokesmen for EDC suggest Canadian content to be in the order of 80 per cent for the corporation's activities in 1979. Suppliers are contacted at least two levels down from the last point of manufacture, and audits are used where questionable estimates are provided. The EDC has found no problems in policing their stringent requirements and have found industry generally cooperative as the process becomes more familiar.

Ontario Hydro "Buy Canadian" Procurement Policy
Description:
Policy to purchase goods of Canadian origin provided that a suitable product is available at a competitive price.

- Foreign firms restricted from bidding list unless:
  1. there is no price competition or price discipline in Canada

    2. equipment required reflects technology only or best available in foreign firms
- Domestic firms *may* be chosen even at a price premium:
    1. intangible benefits assessed, such as less expediting, less tracing of shipments, long-term security of supply, availability of repair and servicing facilities or less risk to Ontario Hydro
    2. 10 per cent price penalty is applied on all reported foreign content

Application:
Canadian preference is only applied when the benefits of doing so are clearly evident.

- Suppliers required to break down Canadian content:
    – manufacturing, labour, engineering
    – raw materials, source of components
- In 1978, of 93,000 purchase orders, 3,000 represented major purchases, "Buy Canadian" policy considered 33 times, and applied 29 times.
- Premiums paid as a result of policy totalled $560,000 or 3/10 of 1 per cent of total purchases.

Foothills (Yukon) Pipe Lines "Buy Canadian" Procurement Policy
Description:
To obtain services and equipment required for the project on a *generally competitive* basis.

- Open and international bid list
- But bids evaluated against other criteria:
    1. to source and purchase equipment and services in Canada by selecting suppliers who have a *substantial* level of technological and innovative input by Canadians
    2. to increase participation of firms substantially owned and controlled by Canadians
    3. to encourage industrial activity throughout Canada
    4. to encourage companies to purchase goods and services in Canada for world-wide operations
    5. to encourage industrial offsets in Canada where foreign goods and services are used
- No percentage penalties are applied.

Application:
Subjective judgement based on ability to satisfy above criteria for contracts valued at over $100,000.

- "Generally competitive" and "substantial level" are left undefined.

90

- Suppliers are required to break out Canadian content:
  - factory costs
  - distribution
  - service
  - sales and administration
  - engineering and development
  - royalties
  - duties, taxes, profits
  - ownership
  - man-years of employment

APPENDIX TABLE 1
PROCUREMENT POLICY: VARIOUS UTILITIES

Utility	Premium Allowed	Preference Shown
Newfoundland & Labrador Hydro	none	Newfoundland
Churchill Falls Corporation	none	Newfoundland
Nova Scotia Power Corporation	none	Nova Scotia
New Brunswick Power Corporation	none	encourage New Brunswick manufacturers to be put on bidding list
Hydro Quebec	10% Quebec 5% Canadian	encourage plant location in Quebec
Ontario Hydro	10% Canadian 3% local	Canadian
Manitoba	none published	Manitoba first
Alberta Power Limited	none published	Alberta first
B.C. Hydro	10% B.C. 5% Canadian	B.C. first

Source: Electrical Association of Canada.

Notes

Chapter 1

[1] Oil, gas and coal supply and reserves figures in this overview are taken from Canadian Petroleum Association, *Statistical Handbook*, 1978.

[2] Excluding natural gas discoveries in the Mackenzie Delta, Beaufort sea and High Arctic which currently have no transmission or marketing facilities. Including these reserves would add another 500 million m³ and yield a 41 per cent increase in reserves over 1969.

[3] J. Philip Prince, *Enhanced Oil Recovery Potential in Canada*, Canadian Energy Research Institute, Study No. 9, March 1980.

[4] Department of Energy, Mines and Resources, *Electric Power in Canada*, Report 78-5, 1978.

[5] Department of Energy, Mines and Resources, *Financing Energy Self-reliance*, EP 77-8, 1977. The estimate is based on two scenarios: high frontier versus high tar sands activity, with the principal assumption being energy self-reliance with net oil imports of no more than 33 per cent of total oil consumption.

[6] A. E. Ames, "Operation Energy: Financing Poses \$350 Billion Task," *Globe & Mail* , 20 March 1980. The estimate is based on two scenarios: low and high, with the principal assumption being energy self-sufficiency with no oil imports.

[7] Canadian Petroleum Association, *Position Paper Regarding Canada's Oil Policy Options* (Calgary, 1979). Oil and gas industry only, no distribution included. The principal assumption: self-sufficient in oil by 1990, primarily because of rapid frontier development.

[8] Bruce Willson, "An Analysis of Canadian Energy Policy and Proposals for Change," the Canadian Institute for Economic Policy, unpublished manuscript, Ottawa, 1979.

Chapter 2

[1] At the time of writing, the Specifications Board of Canada is examining these issues through the Committee for the Identification of Canadian Made Products, representing federal and provincial governments, manufacturers and associations. Its objective is to develop guidelines which manufacturers may use in labelling their products as distinctly Canadian.

[2] Canadian Petroleum Association, *Statistical Handbook*, 1978.

[3] Leonard and Partners Ltd., *Economic Impact of Nuclear Industry in Canada,* for the Canadian Nuclear Association, September 1978.

[4] Department of Industry, Trade and Commerce, *Canadian Nuclear Industry Study,* 1974.

[5] J. A. Douglas, "Nuclear Manufacturing—A Year of Decisions," address to the Canadian Nuclear Association Annual Conference, 1978.

[6] Canadian Nuclear Association, Economic Development Committee, *Nuclear Energy—Its Growth and Impact on the Canadian Economy,* 1975.

[7] Ontario Royal Commission on Electric Power Planning, *Concepts, Conclusions and Recommendations,* vol. 1, 1980.

[8] P. J. W. Pickerill, "Overview of the 1979 Statistical Profile Survey of the Canadian Nuclear Association," address to Nineteenth Annual International Conference, 1979.

[9] Syncrude Canada Ltd., *Environmental Impact Assessment Addendum to the 1973 Report,* vol. A, Summary, November 1978.

[10] See: Alberta Advanced Education and Manpower, *The Construction Industry: Activity, Labour, Demand and Supply, Alberta 1976-1987* (Edmonton, 1978); Esso Resources Canada Ltd., Cold Lake Project, *Socio-Economic Impact Assessment,* vol. III (October 1979); Hobart, Walsh and Associate Consultants Ltd., H. Harries and Associates Ltd., *Social Impact—Benefit/Cost Analysis for Alsands Project Group,* 1979.

[11] Canadian Petroleum Association, *Statistical Profile,* 1978.

[12] Pallister Resource Management Ltd., *Steering a Course to Excellence: A Study of the Canadian Offshore Oil and Gas Service Industries* (Ottawa: National Research Council of Canada, 1977). This report was used extensively in reporting these gaps. See also Department of Industry, Trade and Commerce, *A Report by the Sector Task Force on the Canadian Ocean Industry,* 1978.

Chapter 3

[1] Export Promotion Review Committee, Chairman: Roger Hatch, *Strengthening Canada Abroad* (Ottawa: Department of Industry, Trade and Commerce, November 1979), p. 14.

[2] Department of Industry, Trade and Commerce, *A Report by the Sector Task Force on the Canadian Electrical Industry,* 1978.

DATE DUE